PROBLEM SOLVING AND PYTHON PROGRAMMING

DR. A. POOBALAN | DR SIVAKAMI RAJA | MR S. GOKUL PRAN | MR A. SRINIVASAN | MR M.AROCKIA IRUDAYARAJA

Made with ♥ on the Notion Press Platform
www.notionpress.com

THIS BOOK IS DEDICATED TO LORD SHIRDI SAI BABA AND MY MOTHER P.BALANAGAMMAL FOR OUR ENDLESS SUPPORT.

Contents

Contents

Foreword

The great thing about this book is how well the content is presented. Each chapter is clearly presented. The code examples are all concise, well constructed, and to the point. The exercises are instructive, and any problems you run into will not be at all insurmountable. Your biggest risk is typographical errors. Make it through this book, and you'll definitely no longer be a beginner at Python.

The book is constructed as a series of over fifty exercises, each building on the previous, and each teaching you some new feature of the language. Starting from Exercise 0, getting Python set up on your computer, you begin writing simple programs. You learn about variables, data types, functions, logic, loops, lists, debugging, dictionaries, object-oriented programming, inheritance, and packaging. You even create a simple game using a game engine.

This material covered with five chapters which are summerised below,

1.COMPUTATIONAL THINKING AND PROBLEM SOLVING

2.DATA TYPES, EXPRESSIONS, STATEMENTS

3.CONTROL FLOW, FUNCTIONS, STRINGS

4.LIST TUPLES AND DICTIONARIES

5.FILES, MODULES, PACKAGES

This book is well structured and defined to provide the necessary information for the Python Programming.

Preface

Python is probably one of the few programming languages which is both simple and powerful. This is good for beginners as well as for experts, and more importantly, is fun to program with. This book aims to help you learn this wonderful language and show how to get things done quickly and painlessly - in effect 'The Anti-venom to your programming problems'.

The materials available with the listed reference books have a significant impact on this book. I am greatefully indebted to the authors and publishers of this book and the reference books.

Acknowledgements

My wholehearted and sincere thanks to the "ALMIGHTY" for enabling me to do my task successfully.

This Book was carried out in the Department of Computer Science and Engineering, Sree Vidyanikethan Engineering College,Tirupati. Numerous souls have given a lot of encouragement during this work directly or indirectly contributed to its success. It is my privilege to express my gratitude to all of them.

Most of all, I would like to express my sincere gratitude to my sister Dr S.JEYASUDHA, Professor, EEE Department, K.Ramakrishnan College of Technology, Trichy, for his directions and supports.

I gratefully acknowledge, Dr.A.Poobalan,Assistant Professor,Department of Computer Science and Engineering, University College of Engineering Dindigul,Tamilnadu. Dr.Sivakami Raja, Professor, Department of Computer Science and Engineering, Rajalakshmi Engineering College, Chennai, Mr.S.Gokul Pran, Assistant Professor, Department of Computer Science and Engineering, Mohan Babu University, (Formerly Sree Vidyanikethan Engineering College), Tirupati, Andhrapradesh. Mr A.Srinivasan, Department of Computer Science and Engineering, Velammal College of Engineering and Technology, Madurai. Mr.M.Arockia rudayaraja, Assistant Professor, Department of Computer Science and Engineering, NPR College of Engineering Technology, Natham, for their valuable help and suggestions.

I would like to thank Ms.M.Hafeeza Taj Department of Computer Science and Engineering, Sree Vidyanikethan Engineering College, Tirupati, Andhrapradesh. for help to edit this book.

Finally, I would like to express my deepest gratitude to my father, my mother Mrs. P. Balanagammal and my wife Mrs. T.Nagalakshmi and my son G.Gurusharan & G.Jeevith for their endless support and my brothers Mr.S.Muruganantham (late) and Mr. S. Muralikumar for their support, advice and encouragement. My thanks are due to all my family members and kind-hearted souls who directly or indirectly contributed to the progress of this book.

Syllabus

COURSE OBJECTIVES:

- To understand the basics of algorithmic problem solving.
- To learn to solve problems using Python conditionals and loops.
- To define Python functions and use function calls to solve problems. To use Python data structures – lists, tuples, dictionaries to represent complex data.
- To do input/output with files in Python.

UNIT I COMPUTATIONAL THINKING AND PROBLEM SOLVING

Fundamentals of Computing – Identification of Computational Problems -Algorithms, building blocks of algorithms (statements, state, control flow, functions), notation (pseudo code, flow chart, programming language), algorithmic problem solving, simple strategies for developing algorithms (iteration, recursion). Illustrative problems: find minimum in a list, insert a card in a list of sorted cards, guess an integer number in a range, Towers of Hanoi.

UNIT II DATA TYPES, EXPRESSIONS, STATEMENTS

Python interpreter and interactive mode, debugging; values and types: int, float, boolean, string, and list; variables, expressions, statements, tuple assignment, precedence of operators, comments; Illustrative programs: exchange the values of two variables, circulate the values of n variables, distance between two points.

UNIT III CONTROL FLOW, FUNCTIONS, STRINGS

Conditionals: Boolean values and operators, conditional (if), alternative (if-else), chained conditional (if-elif-else); Iteration: state, while, for, break, continue, pass; Fruitful functions: return values, parameters, local and global scope, function composition, recursion; Strings: string slices, immutability, string functions and methods, string module; Lists as arrays. Illustrative programs: square root, gcd, exponentiation, sum an array of numbers, linear search, binary search.

UNIT IV LISTS, TUPLES, DICTIONARIES

Lists: list operations, list slices, list methods, list loop, mutability, aliasing, cloning lists, list parameters; Tuples: tuple assignment, tuple as return value; Dictionaries: operations and methods; advanced list processing – list comprehension; Illustrative programs: simple sorting, histogram, Students marks statement, Retail bill preparation.

UNIT V FILES, MODULES, PACKAGES

Files and exception: text files, reading and writing files, format operator; command line arguments, errors and exceptions, handling exceptions, modules, packages; Illustrative programs: word count, copy file, Voter's age validation, Marks range validation (0-100).

COURSE OUTCOMES:

Upon completion of the course, students will be able to

CO1: Develop algorithmic solutions to simple computational problems.
CO2: Develop and execute simple Python programs.
CO3: Write simple Python programs using conditionals and looping for solving problems.
CO4: Decompose a Python program into functions.
CO5: Represent compound data using Python lists, tuples, dictionaries etc.
CO6: Read and write data from/to files in Python programs.

CHAPTER ONE

COMPUTATIONAL THINKING AND PROBLEM SOLVING

1.1.Fundamentals of Computing

Computer is an advanced electronic device that takes raw data as an input from the user and processes it under the control of a set of instructions (called program), produces a result (output), and saves it for future use.In order to carry out its operations, a computer system is divided into three separate units. They are: 1) Arithmetic logical unit, 2) Control unit, and 3) Central processing unit. All these three units are known as functional units.

i) Arithmetic Logical Unit (ALU)-The processing of the data and instructions are performed by Arithmetic Logical Unit. The major operations performed by the ALU are addition, subtraction, multiplication, division, logic and comparison .For processing, data is transferred from storage unit to ALU. After processing, the output is returned back to storage unit for further processing or for storing purpose.

ii)Control Unit (CU)- The next component of computer is the Control Unit, which acts like the supervisor seeing that things are done in proper way. The control unit determines the sequence in which computer programs and instructions are to be executed. Activities like processing of programs stored in the main memory, interpretation of the instructions and issuing of signals for other units of the computer to execute them are carried out by CU. It coordinates the activities of computer's peripheral equipment which include input and output devices. Therefore, it is the manager of all the operations mentioned in the previous section.

iii)Central Processing Layout(CPU) -The ALU and the CU of a computer system are jointly known as the central processing unit(CPU) . You may call CPU as the brain of any computer system. It is just like brain that takes all major decisions, makes all sorts of calculations and directs different parts of the computer functions by activating and controlling the operations. The CPU (Central Processing Unit) is the device that interprets and executes instructions.

1.2.Identification of Computational Problems

In theoretical computer science, a computational problem is a problem that may be solved by an algorithm. In todays world we face many computational problems and identification of those problems is very important as they make finding solution which is easier and can be implemented easily. There are some types in computational problems and they are described below:

1)Decision Problems - A decision problem is a computational problem where the answer for every instance is either yes or no. An example of a decision problem is primality testing: "Given a positive integer n, determine if n is prime." A decision problem is typically represented as the set of all instances for which the answer is *yes*. For example, primality testing can be represented as the infinite set $L = \{2, 3, 5, 7, 11, ...\}$

2)Search Problems - In a search problem, the answers can be arbitrary strings. For example, factoring is a search problem where the instances are (string representations of) positive integers and the solutions are (string representations of) collections of primes. A search problem is represented as a relation consisting of all the instance-solution pairs, called a search relation. For example, factoring can be represented as the relation $R = \{(4, 2), (6, 2), (6, 3), (8, 2), (9, 3), (10, 2), (10, 5)...\}$ which consist of all pairs of numbers (n, p), where p is a nontrivial prime factor of n.

Problem Solving Techniques:

Problem solving can be expressed in the form of

1.Algorithms. 2.Flowcharts. 3.Pseudo codes. 4.Programs

1.3.Algorithm

The word **Algorithm** means " A set of finite rules or instructions to be followed in calculations or other problem-solving operations " Or " A procedure for solving a mathematical problem in a finite number of steps that frequently involves recursive operations".Algorithms help to do a task in programming to get the expected output. The Algorithm designed are language-independent, i.e. they are just plain instructions that can be implemented in any language, and yet the output will be the same, as expected.

In order for some instructions to be an algorithm, it must have the following characteristics (as in fig 1.3.1):

- **Clear and Unambiguous:** The algorithm should be clear and unambiguous. Each of its steps should be clear in all aspects and must lead to only one meaning.
- **Well-Defined Inputs:** If an algorithm says to take inputs, it should be well-defined inputs. It may or may not take input.
- **Well-Defined Outputs:** The algorithm must clearly define what output will be yielded and it should be well-defined as well. It should produce at least 1 output.
- **Finite-ness:** The algorithm must be finite, i.e. it should terminate after a finite time.
- **Feasible:** The algorithm must be simple, generic, and practical, such that it can be executed with the available resources. It must not contain some future technology or anything.
- **Language Independent:** The Algorithm designed must be language-independent, i.e. it must be just plain instructions that can be implemented in any language, and yet the output will be the same, as expected.

There are so many methods or logics available to solve the problem individually. All of those methods and logics may not be good, for given problem there may be so many algorithms not of all equality. The following are the primary factors that are oftenly used to judge the quality of the algorithms.

1.3.1Factors - Quality of good Algorithm

1. Time - To execute a program, the computer system takes some amount of time. The lesser is the time required, the better is the algorithm.

2. Memory - To execute a program, computer system takes some amount of memory storage. The lesser is the memory required, the better is the algorithm.

3. Accuracy - Multiple algorithms may provide suitable or correct solutions to a given problem, some of these may provide more accurate results than others, such algorithms may be suitable.

4. Sequence - The procedure of an algorithm must form in a sequence and some of the instruction of an algorithm may be repeated in number of times of until a particular condition is met.

5. Generability - The designed algorithm must solve isolated problem and more often algorithms are designed to handle a range of input data to meet this criteria, so the algorithms must be generalised.

Example-1:

Write an algorithm to print „Good Morning”

Step 1: Start **Step 2:** Print “Good Morning” **Step 3:** Stop

Example-2: algorithm to multiply 2 numbers and print the result:

Step 1: *Start*

Step 2: *Get the knowledge of input. Here we need 3 variables; a and b will be the user input and c will hold the result.*

Step 3: *Declare a, b, c variables.*

Step 4: *Take input for a and b variable from the user.*
Step 5: *Know the problem and find the solution using operators, data structures and logic.We need to multiply a and b variables so we use * operator and assign the result to c.*
*That is c <- a * b*

Step 6: *Check how to give output, Here we need to print the output. So write print c*

Step 7: *End.*

1.4 Building Blocks of Algorithms:

Algorithms can be constructed from basic building blocks namely, sequence, selection and iteration.Algorithm is defined as the effective step-by-step procedure to solve the problem in a finite number of steps. Algorithms can be designed using the components . They are:

i)Instructions/Statements

ii)State

iii)Control Flow

iv) Functions

1.4.1 Instructions/ Statements:

Statement may be a single action in a computer.In a computer statements might include some of the following actions:

- Input data-information given to the program.
- process data-perform operation on a given input.
- output data-processed result.

1.4.2 State

State is defined as the condition of algorithm at a moment in a time.Transition from one process to another process under specified condition with in a time is called state.

Algorithm can be in any of the following states.

Fig-2:States of an Algorithm

1. START state :It represents the starting of the program.

2. INPUT state:It represents the process of reading the input from the user.

3. PROCESS state:It represents the process done in the program. E.g. Addition, Subtraction etc..

4. OUTPUT state:It represents the output displayed on the screen.

5. STOP state:It represents the ending of the program.

Example: Algorithm to find the sum of two numbers.

a. Start (START state)

b. Read A, B (INPUT state)

c. C=A+B (PROCESS state)

d. Print C (OUTPUT state)

e. Stop (STOP state)

1.4.3 Control flow:

The process of executing the statements in the given sequence is called as control flow.

The three ways in executing the control flow are ;

1. Sequence
2. Selection
3. Iteration

Sequence:

The given set of instructions executed consecutively is called sequence execution.

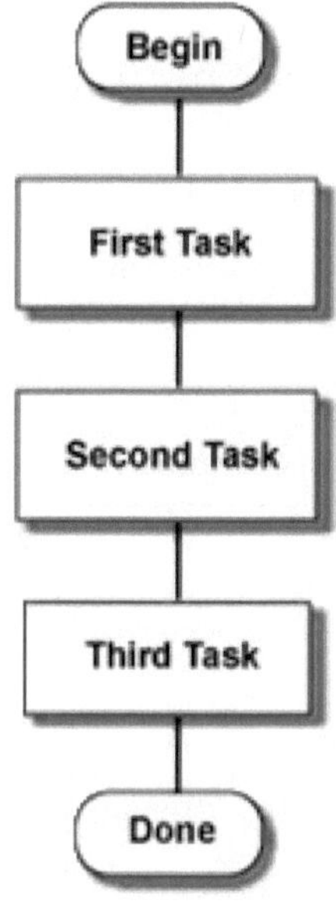

Fig-3:Sequence Flow of Algorithms.

Example: Algorithm to find the average of three numbers, the algorithm is as follows.

Step1: Start
Step2: Get three numbers a, b, c as input
Step3: Find the sum of a, b and c
Step4: Divide the sum by 3
Step5: Store the result in variable d
Step6: Print d
Step7: Stop

The above algorithm finds the average of three numbers a, b and c. The numbers are the input provided by the user .After adding the total is divided by 3 and the result is stored in a variable d and it is printed.

Selection:

A selection statement is transferring the program control to a specific part of the program based upon the condition. If the condition is true, one part of the program will be executed, otherwise the other part of the program will be executed.

Example: Algorithm to find the Largest of two numbers, the algorithm is as follows

Step1: Start

Step 2: Get two numbers a and b as input

Step 3: IF a>b THEN

Step 4: PRINT “A is Large”

Step 5: ELSE PRINT “B is Large”

Step 6: ENDIF

Step 7: Stop

The above algorithm is used to find the Largest of two numbers a and bThe numbers are the input provided by the user .The number a and b are compared, If a is larger Print “A is Large” or if b is larger print “B is Large”.

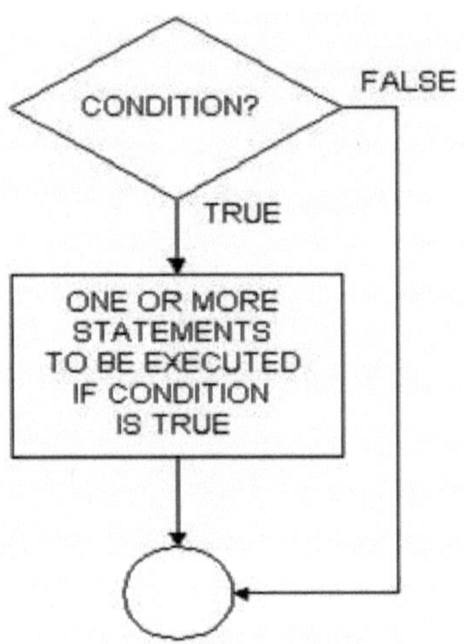

Fig-4:Selection Flow of Algorithms.

Iteration:

Iteration is a type of execution where a certain set of statements are executed again and again based upon condition. This type of execution is also called as looping or repetition.

Example: Algorithm to print all natural numbers up to n, the algorithm is as follows

Step 1: Start

Step 2: Get the value of n.

Step 3: Initialize i=1

Step 4: if (i<=n) go to step 5 else go to step 7

Step 5: Print i value and increment i value by 1

Step 6: Go to step 4

Step 7: Stop

The above algorithm is for printing first n natural numbers .The user provides the input. The first value, i is initialized. A loop is initialized. The first value is printed and the number is incremented. The i value is checked with n, the user input. The numbers are printed until i becomes greater than n.

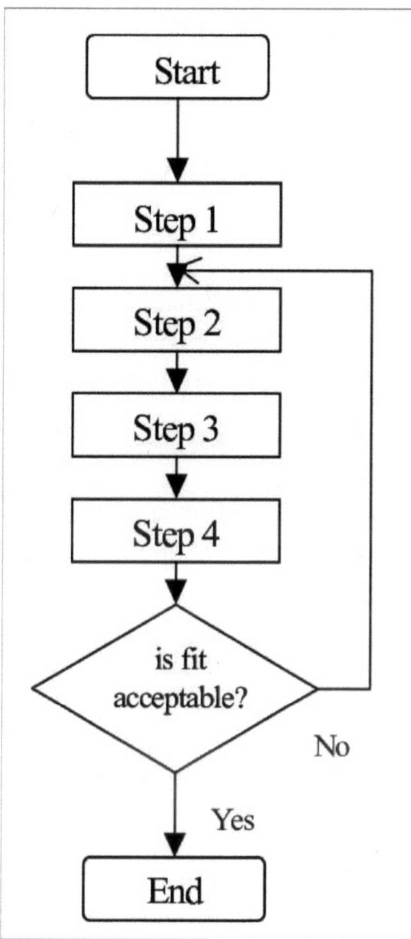

Fig-5:Iteration Flow of Algorithms.

1.4.4 Functions:

Function is a sub program which consists of block of instructions that performs a particular task. For complex problems, the problem is been divided into smaller and simpler tasks during algorithm design.

Benefits of Using Functions are:

- Reduction in line of code
- code reuse

- Better readability
- Information hiding
- Easy to debug and test
- Improved maintainabilit

Example: Algorithm for addition of two numbers using function Main function ()

Step 1: Start

Step 2: Call the function add ()

Step 3: Stop

The above algorithm is to call the function add. This function is called as Main function or calling function.

Subfunction add ()

Step 1: Function start

Step 2: Get two numbers as input and store it in to a and b

Step 3: Add the numbers a & b and store the result in c

Step 4: Print c

Step 5: Return.

The above algorithm is called as the called function which is to add two numbers a and b. The numbers are the input provided by the user .After adding the result is stored in a variable c and it is printed.

1.5 Notation

Notations are form for representation of algorithms. We represent algorithms basically in the below forms:

1.Flow Chart 2.Pseudo Code 3.programming language

All the above methods represent the algorithm in many ways like graphical and some high level languages etc..

1.5.1 Flow Chart

Flowcharts are nothing but the graphical representation of the data or the algorithm for a better understanding of the code visually. It displays step-by-step solutions to a problem, algorithm, or process. It is a pictorial way of representing steps that are preferred by most beginner-level programmers to understand algorithms of computer science.

Symbol	Symbol Name	Description
	Flow Lines	Used to connect symbols
	Terminal	Used to start, pause or halt in the program logic
	Input/output	Represents the information entering or leaving the system
	Processing	Represents arithmetic and logical instructions
	Decision	Represents a decision to be made
	Connector	Used to Join different flow lines
	Sub function	used to call function

Table-1:Shapes for constructing a flow chart

Before we start construction of algorithm we need to follow some rules. This rules are accepted global-wide and used internationally for a graphical representation of an algorithm.

1.5.1.1Rules for Constructing a Flow Chart

1.The flowchart should be clear, neat and easy to follow.

2.The flowchart must have a logical start and finish.

3.Only one flow line should come out from a process symbol.

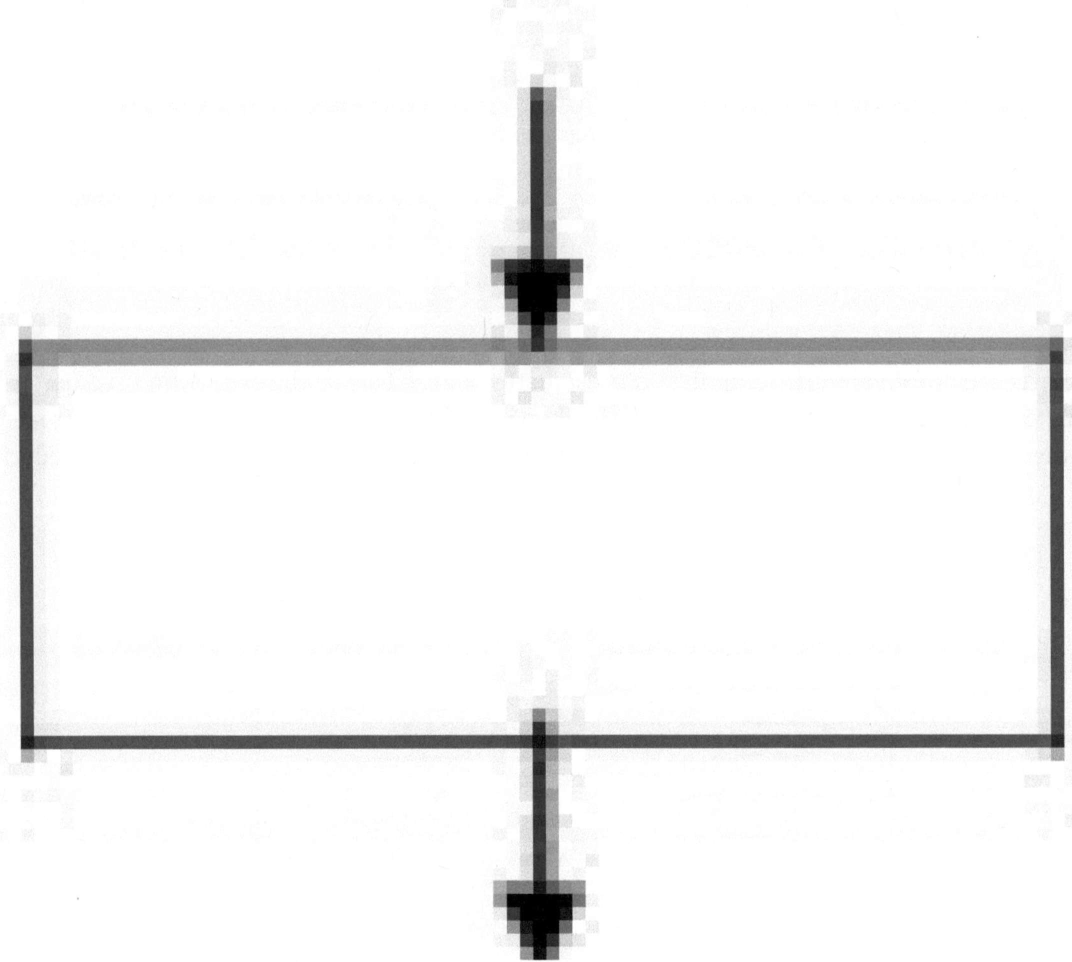

4. Only one flow line should enter a decision symbol. However, two or three flow lines may leave the decision symbol.

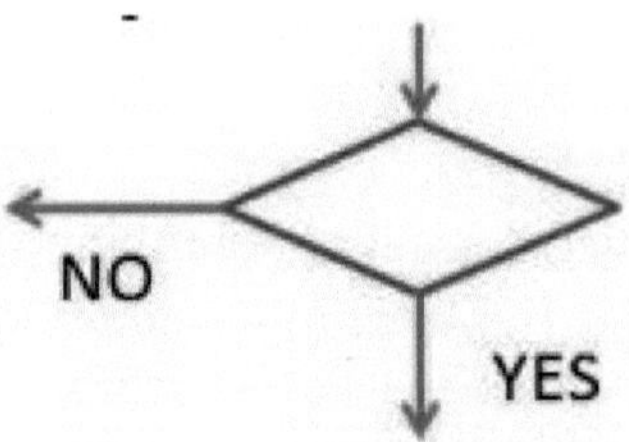

conditional flow representation

5. Only one flow line is used with a terminal symbol.

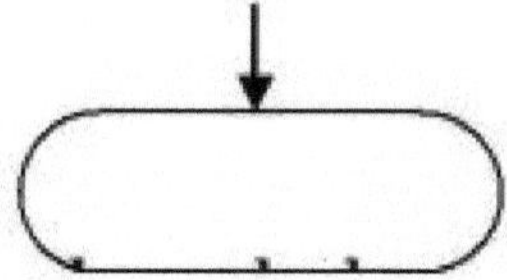

Enter Caption

6. Within standard symbols, write briefly and precisely.

7. Intersection of flow lines should be avoided.

Example-1:Draw a flowchart to find the greatest number among the2 numbers.

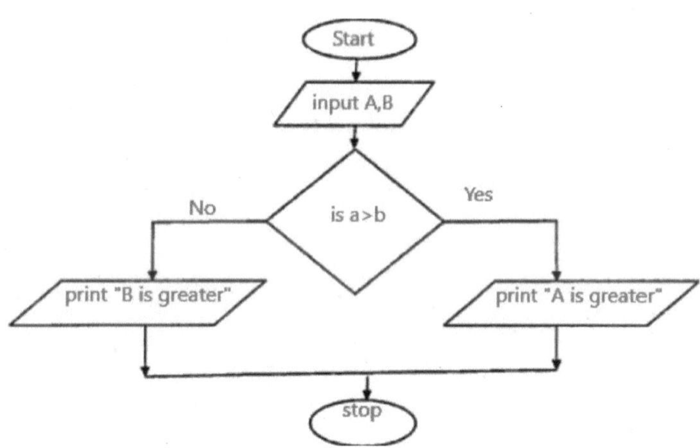

Flow chart to fing greatest among 2

1.5.2 Pseudo Code:

It's simply an implementation of an algorithm in the form of annotations and informative text written in plain English. It has no syntax like any of the programming language and thus can't be compiled or interpreted by the computer. Often at times, algorithms are represented with the help of pseudo codes as they can be interpreted by programmers no matter what their programming background or knowledge is. Pseudo code, as the name suggests, is a false code or a representation of code which can be understood by even a layman with some school level programming knowledge.

1.5.2.1 Rules for writing a Pseudo Code

1.Write one statement per line 2.Capitalize keywords. 3.Indent to hierarchy. 4.Keep statements language independent.

1.5.2.2 Common keywords used in writing a Pseudo code

1.Comment: //

2. BEGIN,END: Begin is the first statement and end is the last statement.

3. **INPUT, GET, READ**: The keyword is used to inputting data.

4. **COMPUTE, CALCULATE**: used for calculation of the result of the given expression.

5. **ADD, SUBTRACT, INITIALIZE** used for addition, subtraction and initialization.

6. **OUTPUT, PRINT, DISPLAY**: It is used to display the output of the program.

7. **IF, ELSE, ENDIF**: used to make decision.

8. **WHILE, ENDWHILE**: used for iterative statements.

9. **FOR, ENDFOR**: Another iterative incremented/decremented tested automatically.

The pseudo code syntaxes for the loops is as written below:

1.Syntax for if else:

IF (condition)THEN statement

ELSE statement ENDIF

Example: Greates of two numbers

BEGIN READ a,b IF (a>b) THEN DISPLAY a is greater

ELSE DISPLAY b is greater END IF END

2.Syntax for For:

FOR(start-value to end-value) DO

statement ENDFOR

Example: Print n natural numbers

BEGIN GET n INITIALIZE i=1

FOR (i<=n) DO PRINT i i=i+1 ENDFOR END

3.Syntax for While:

WHILE (condition) DO

statement

ENDWHILE

Example: Print n natural numbers

BEGIN

GET n

INITIALIZE i=1

WHILE(i<=n) DO

PRINT i

i=i+1

ENDWHILE

END

1.5.3 Programming Language

A programming language is a **computer language** that is used by **programmers (developers) to communicate with computers**. It is a set of instructions written in any specific language (C, C++, Java, Python) to perform a specific task.A programming language is mainly used to **develop desktop applications, websites, and mobile applications.**Types of programming language

1.Machine language 2.Assembly language 3.High level language

1.5.3.1Machine language:

The computer can understand only machine language which uses 0's and 1's. In machine language the different instructions are formed by taking different combinations of 0's and 1's.

1.5.3.2Assembly language:

To overcome the issues in programming language and make the programming process easier, an assembly language is developed which is logically equivalent to machine language but it is easier for people to read, write and understand.

1. Assembly language is symbolic representation of machine language. Assembly languages are symbolic programming language that uses symbolic notation to represent machine language instructions. They are called low level language because they are so closely related to the machines.

Assembler

Assembler is the program which translates assembly language instruction in to a machine language.

1. Easy to understand and use.
2. It is easy to locate and correct errors

1.5.3.3High level language

High level language contains English words and symbols. The specified rules are to be followed while writing program in high level language.

Translating high level language to machine language

The programs that translate high level language in to machine language are called interpreter or compiler.

Compiler:

A compiler is a program which translates the source code written in a high level language in to object code which is in machine language program. Compiler reads the whole program written in high level language and translates it to machine language. If any error is found it display error message on the screen.

Interpreter

Interpreter translates the high level language program in line by line manner. The interpreter translates a high level language statement in a source program to a machine code and executes it immediately before translating the next statement. When an error is found the execution of the program is halted and error message is displayed on the screen.

1.6 Algorithmic Problem Solving

Algorithmic problem solving is solving problem that require the formulation of an algorithm for the solution. Below figure represents the steps for solving a problem.

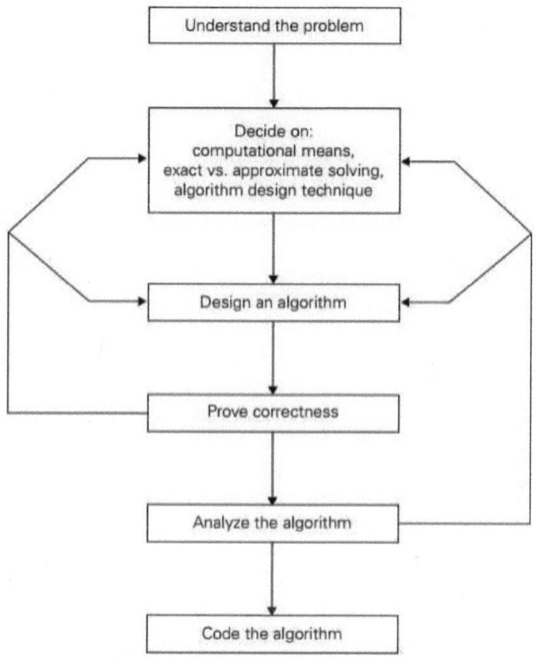

Fig-6: Steps for Algorithmic Problem Solving.

1.Understanding the Problem- It is the process of finding the input of the problem that the algorithm solves. It is very important to specify exactly the set of inputs the algorithm needs to handle

2.Choosing between Exact and Approximate Problem Solving- The next principal decision is to choose between solving the problem exactly or solving it approximately. Based on this, the algorithms are classified as exact *algorithm* and *approximation algorithm.*

3.Deciding a data structure:- Data structure plays a vital role in designing and analysis the algorithms. Some of the algorithm design techniques also depend on the structuring data specifying a problem's instance Algorithm+ Data structure=programs.

4.Algorithm Design Techniques - An *algorithm design technique* (or "strategy" or "paradigm") is a general approach to solving problems algorithmically that is applicable to a variety of problems from different areas of computing.

5.Methods of Specifying an Algorithm - *Pseudocode* is a mixture of a natural language and programming language-like constructs. Pseudocode is usually more precise than natural language, and its usage often yields more succinct algorithm descriptions.

6.Analysing an Algorithm - Efficiency-Time efficiency, indicating how fast the algorithm runs, Space efficiency, indicating how much extra memory it uses. Simplicity- An algorithm should be precisely defined and investigated with mathematical expressions. Simpler algorithms are easier to understand and easier to program. Simple algorithms usually contain fewer bugs.

7.Coding an Algorithm - Most algorithms are destined to be ultimately implemented as computer programs. Programming an algorithm presents both a peril and an opportunity.

1.7 Simple Strategies for Developing Algorithms

There are some simple strategies where we can reuse a code multiple time as we need. There are 2 imporatnt methods:

1.Iterations

A sequence of statements is executed until a specified condition is true is called iterations.

1.for loop

2.While loop

Syntax for For:

FOR(*start-value to end-value*) DO

Statement

...

ENDFOR

Syntax for While:

WHILE (condition) DO

Statement

...

ENDWHILE

2.Recursions

A function that calls itself is known as recursion. Recursion is a process by which a function calls itself repeatedly until some specified condition has been satisfied.Recursion is an amazing technique with the help of which we can reduce the length of our code and make it easier to read and write. It has certain advantages over the iteration technique which will be discussed later. A task that can be defined with its similar subtask, recursion is one of the best solutions for it. For example; The Factorial of a number.

Algorithm for factorial of n numbers using recursion:

Main function:

Step1: Start

Step2: Get n

Step3: call factorial(n)

Step4: print fact

Step5: Stop

Sub function factorial(n):

Step1: if(n==1) then fact=1 return fact

Step2: else fact=n*factorial(n-1) and return fact

1.8 ILLUSTRATIVE PROBLEMS

1. Guess an integer in a range

Algorithm:

Step1: Start

Step 2: Declare hidden, guess

Step 3: Compute hidden= Choose a random value in a range

Step 4: Read guess

Step 5: If guess=hidden, then

Print Guess is hit

Else

Print Guess not hit

Print hidden

Step 6: Stop

2. Find minimum in a list

Algorithm:

Step 1: Start

Step 2: Read n

Step 3:Initialize i=0

Step 4: If i<n, then goto

step 4.1, 4.2 else goto

step 5 Step4.1: Read a[i]

Step 4.2: i=i+1 goto step 4

Step 5: Compute min=a[0]

Step 6: Initialize i=1

Step 7: If i<n, then go to step 8 else goto step 10

Step 8: If a[i]<min, then goto

step 8.1,8.2 else goto 8.2

Step 8.1: min=a[i]

Step 8.2: i=i+1 goto 7

Step 9: Print min

Step 10: Stop

3. Tower of Hanoi

Algorithm:

Step 1: Start

Step 2: Read n

Step 3: Calculate move=pow(2,n)-1

Step 4: Function call T(n,Beg,Aux,End) recursively until n=0

Step 4.1: If n=0, then goto

step 5 else goto step

4.2 Step

4.2: T(n-1,Beg,End,Aux) T(1,Beg,Aux,End) , Move disk from source to desti ation T(n-1,Aux,Beg,End)

Step 5: Stop

CHAPTER TWO

DATA TYPES, EXPRESSIONS, STATEMENTS

Introduction

Python is a high-level, general-purpose programming language. Its design philosophy emphasizes code readability with the use of significant indentation. Python is dynamically-typed and garbage-collected. It supports multiple programming paradigms, including structured (particularly procedural), object-oriented and functional programming. It is often described as a "batteries included" language due to its comprehensive standard library.

- Python is Open Source which means its available free of cost.
- Python is simple and so easy to learn
- Python is versatile and can be used to create many different things.
- Python has powerful development libraries include AI, ML etc.
- Python is much in demand and ensures high salary

Python has a large and active community that contributes to Python's pool of modules and libraries, and acts as a helpful resource for other programmers. The vast support community means that if coders run into a stumbling block, finding a solution is relatively easy; somebody is bound to have encountered the same problem before.

2.1 Python Interpreter

Interpreter is used to execute a program in a high-level language by translating it one line at a time.Compiler is used to translate a program written in a high-level language into a low-level language all at once, in preparation for later execution.

Compiler	Interpreter
Compiler Takes **Entire** program as input	Interpreter Takes **Single** instruction as input
Intermediate Object Code is **Generated**	**No** Intermediate Object Code is **Generated**
Conditional Control Statements are Executes **faster**	Conditional Control Statements are Executes **slower**
Memory Requirement is **More**(Since Object Code is Generated)	**Memory Requirement** is **Less**
Program need not be **compiled** every time	Every time higher level program is converted into lower level program
Errors are displayed after **entire program** is checked	**Errors** are displayed for **every instruction** interpreted (if any)
Example : C Compiler	**Example** : PYTHON

Table-1: Difference between Compiler and Interpreter.

The interpreter's line-editing features usually aren't very sophisticated. On Unix, whoever installed the interpreter may have enabled support for the GNU readline library, which adds more elaborate interactive editing and history features. Perhaps the quickest check to see whether command line editing is supported is typing Control-P to the first Python prompt you get. For example, what happens if you use + with strings or with lists? Here is an interpreter session trying + that way. The >>> is the prompt, the bold text is what you type, followed by the interpreter's response on the next line.

>>> 'hello' + '!' 'hello!' >>> [1, 2] + [3, 4] [1, 2, 3, 4] >>>

You could look up the formal description of +, but just typing an experiment in the interpreter to see what it does is quick and satisfying. Incidentally, examples like the above are used throughout these pages to show phrases of Python code with their output. You can always start your own interpreter session to replicate and play with these experiments yourself.

Working With The Interpreter

The interpreter prints a >>> prompt and waits for you to type some Python code. It reads what you type, evaluates it, and prints the result — the so called read-eval-print loop (here what the user types is shown in bold)

>>> 1 + 2 * 3 7 >>> ‘hello’ + ’there‘ ’hellothere‘ >>> max(1, 5, -2) 5 >>> ’hello‘ + 2 TypeError: can only concatenate str (not "int") to str >>> ’hello‘ + str(2) ’hello2' >>>

This is an excellent way to experiment with Python features to see how they work. If you have some code you are thinking about, it can be quick and informative to fire up the interpreter, and type the code in to see what it does. When you write a Python program, you store your code in a file like hello.py, where you can write and revise a series of functions and comments and whatnot over many lines, like writing a paper. You would not want to write a whole program at the >>> prompt, which works best for little throw-away phrases.

2.2 Modes of Python Interpreter:

Python Interpreter is a program that reads and executes Python code. It uses 2 modes of Execution.

1.Interactive mode 2.Script mode

1. Interactive mode:

Interactive Mode, as the name suggests, allows us to interact with OS. When we type a Python statement, the interpreter displays the result(s) immediately. Interactive mode is a good way to play around and try variations on syntax. On macOS or linux, open a terminal and simply type "python". On Windows, bring up the command prompt and type "py", or start an interactive Python session by selecting "Python (command line)", "IDLE", or similar program from the task bar / app menu. IDLE is a GUI which includes both an interactive mode and options to edit and run files.

Advantages:

Python, in interactive mode, is good enough to learn, experiment or explore. Working in interactive mode is convenient for beginners and for testing small pieces of code.

Drawback:

We cannot save the statements and have to retype all the statements once again to re-run them. In interactive mode, you type Python programs and the interpreter displays the result:

The chevron, >>>, is the prompt the interpreter uses to indicate that it is ready for you to enter code. If you type 1 + 1, the interpreter replies 2.

>>> print ('Hello, World!') >>>1 + 1 Hello, World!

This is an example of a print statement. It displays a result on the screen. In this case, the result is the words.

2. Script mode:

In script mode, we type python program in a file and then use an interpreter to execute the content of the file. Scripts can be saved to disk for future use. Python scripts have the extension .py, meaning that the filename ends with .py Save the code with **filename.py** and run the interpreter in script mode to execute the script. Instead of Python exiting when the program is finished, you can use the -i flag to start an interactive session. This can be **very** useful for debugging and prototyping.

Example1:

```
print(1)
x = 2
print(x)
```

Output:

```
>>>1
   2
```

Interactive mode	Script mode
A way of using the Python interpreter by typing commands and expressions at the prompt.	A way of using the Python interpreter to read and execute statements in a script.
Cant save and edit the code	Can save and edit the code
If we want to experiment with the code, we can use interactive mode.	If we are very clear about the code, we can use script mode.
we cannot save the statements for further use and we have to retype all the statements to re-run them.	we can save the statements for further use and we no need to retype all the statements to re-run them.
We can see the results immediately.	We cant see the code immediately.

Table-2: Differences between the python interactive Modes.

Integrated Development Learning Environment (IDLE):

Is a graphical user interface which is completely written in Python. It is bundled with the default implementation of the python language and also comes with optional part of the Python packaging.

Features of IDLE:

Multi-window text editor with syntax highlighting. Auto completion with smart indentation. Python shell to display output with syntax highlighting.

2.3 Debugging in Python

Debugging in Python is facilitated by pdb module (python debugger) which comes built-in to the Python standard library. It is actually defined as the class Pdb which internally makes use of bdb(basic debugger functions) and cmd (support for line-oriented command interpreters) modules.

pdb supports:

- Setting breakpoints ,Stepping through code,Source code listing,Viewing stack traces

The debugger is extensible – it is actually defined as the class Pdb. This is currently undocumented but easily understood by reading the source. The extension interface uses the modules bdb and cmd.

The debugger's prompt is (Pdb). Typical usage to run a program under control of the debugger is:

>>> **importpdb**

>>> **importmymodule**

>>> **pdb.run('mymodule.test()')**

For example: **python3 -m pdb myscript.py**

When invoked as a script, pdb will automatically enter post-mortem debugging if the program being debugged exits abnormally. Automatic restarting preserves pdb's state (such as breakpoints) and in most cases is more useful than quitting the debugger upon program's exit.

The typical usage to inspect a crashed program is:

>>> **importpdb**

>>> **importmymodule**

>>> mymodule.test()

The module defines the following functions; each enters the debugger in a slightly different way:

1.pdb.run(*statement, globals=None, locals=None*) : Execute the *statement* (given as a string or a code object) under debugger control. The optional *globals* and *locals* arguments specify the environment in which the code is executed; by default the dictionary of the module __main__ is used. (See the explanation of the built-in exec() or eval() functions.)

2.pdb.runeval(*expression, globals=None, locals=None*) : Evaluate the *expression* (given as a string or a code object) under debugger control. When runeval() returns, it returns the value of the expression. Otherwise this function is similar to run().

3.pdb.runcall(*function, *args, **kwds*) : Call the *function* (a function or method object, not a string) with the given arguments. When runcall() returns, it returns whatever the function call returned. The debugger prompt appears as soon as the function is entered.

4.pdb.set_trace(*, *header=None*) : Enter the debugger at the calling stack frame. This is useful to hard-code a breakpoint at a given point in a program, even if the code is not otherwise being debugged (e.g. when an assertion fails). If given, *header* is printed to the console just before debugging begins.

5.pdb.post_mortem(*traceback=None*) : Enter post-mortem debugging of the given *traceback* object. If no *traceback* is given, it uses the one of the exception that is currently being handled (an exception must be being handled if the default is to be used).

Debugger Commands

The commands recognized by the debugger are listed below. Most commands can be abbreviated to one or two letters as indicated; e.g. h(elp) means that either h or help can be used to enter the help command (but not he or hel, nor H or Help or HELP). Arguments to commands must be separated by whitespace (spaces or tabs).

help[command] ; Without argument, print the list of available commands. With a *command* as argument, print help about that command. help pdb displays the full documentation (the docstring of the pdb module). Since the *command* argument must be an identifier, help exec must be entered to get help on the ! command.

where : Print a stack trace, with the most recent frame at the bottom. An arrow indicates the current frame, which determines the context of most commands.

down [count] : Move the current frame *count* (default one) levels down in the stack trace (to a newer frame).

up [count] : Move the current frame *count* (default one) levels up in the stack trace (to an older frame).

clear [filename:lineno | bpnumber ...] : With a *filename:lineno* argument, clear all the breakpoints at this line. With a space separated list of breakpoint numbers, clear those breakpoints. Without argument, clear all breaks (but first ask confirmation).

2.4 Values and Types

Value can be any letter ,number or string.A value is one of the most basic things in any program works with. A value may be characters i.e. 'Hello, World!' or a number like 1,2.2 ,3.5 etc.Values belong to different types: 1 is an integer, 2 is a float and 'Hello, World!' is a string etc.Python supports 3 types of numbers: integers, float and complex number.If you want to know what type a value has you can use type() function. Paste the following code and click the run button to check the output.These values (1, 2, and "Hello, World!") belong to different types in Python programming: 1, 2 are integers, and "Hello, World!" is a string, so called because it contains a "string" of letters.

Example:

>>> x=type('Hello, World!') print(x) <class 'str' >>> y=type(17)

print(y) #returns <class 'int'> <class 'int'>

Now we shift our concentration towards Data types that pyhton supports.

Data Types

A data type, in programming, is a classification that specifies which type of value a variable has and what type of mathematical, relational or logical operations can be applied to it without causing an error When a programming language allows a variable of one data type to be used as if it were a value of another data type, the language is said to be *weakly typed*. Technically, the concept of a *strongly typed* or *weakly typed* programming language is a fallacy. In every programming language, all values of a variable have a static type -- but the type might be one whose values are classified into one or more classes.

Python has five standard data types:

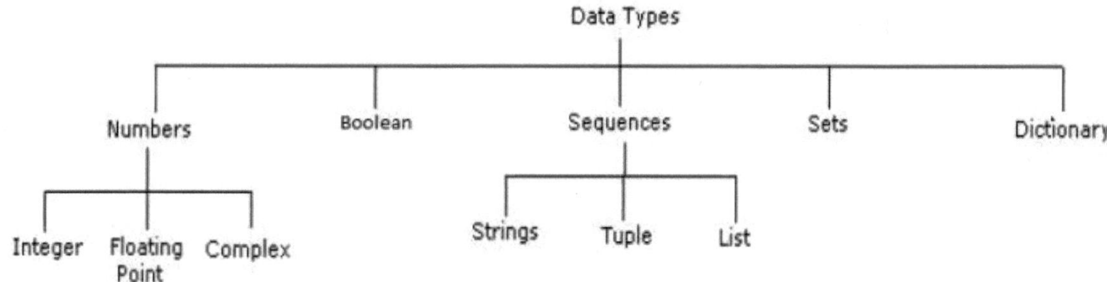

Fig-Describing Data types in python programming

1. Python Numeric Data Type

Python numeric data type is used to hold numeric values like;

1. int - holds signed integers of non-limited length.
2. long- holds long integers(exists in Python 2.x, deprecated in Python 3.x).
3. float- holds floating precision numbers and it's accurate up to 15 decimal places.
4. complex- holds complex numbers.

Number data type stores Numerical Values. This data type is immutable [i.e. values/items cannot be changed].

- **Integers** – This value is represented by int class. It contains positive or negative whole numbers (without fraction or decimal). In Python there is no limit to how long an integer value can be.

- **Float** – This value is represented by float class. It is a real number with floating point representation. It is specified by a decimal point. Optionally, the character e or E followed by a positive or negative integer may be appended to specify scientific notation.

- **Complex Numbers** – Complex number is represented by complex class. It is specified as *(real part) + (imaginary part)j.* For example – 2+3j

Note – type() function is used to determine the type of data type.

The difference all of the numeric types is as stated as below in table

Integers	Long	Float	Complex
- They are often called just integers or **int**. - They are positive or negative whole numbers with no decimal point.	-They are long integers. -They can also be represented in octal and hexadecimal representation.	-They are written with a decimal point dividing the integer and the fractional parts.	-They are of the form **a + bj**, where a and b are floats and j represents the square root of -1 (which is an imaginary number). -The real part of the number is a, and the imaginary part is b.
Eg, 56	**Eg, 5692431L**	**Eg, 56.778**	**Eg, square root of-1 is a complex number**

Table-Differences in Numeric data types.

2.Sequence:

A sequence is an ordered collection of items, indexed by positive integers. It is a combination of mutable (value can be changed) and immutable (values cannot be changed) data types. There are three types of sequence data type available in Python, they are

1.Strings 2.Lists 3.Tuples

1) String

In Python, Strings are arrays of bytes representing Unicode characters. A string is a collection of one or more characters put in a single quote, double-quote or triple quote. In python there is no character data type, a character is a string of length one. It is represented by str class. Basically a String in Python consists of a series or sequence of characters - letters, numbers, and special characters. Strings are marked by quotes:

single quotes (' ') Eg, 'This a string in single quotes' double quotes (" ") Eg, "'This a string in double quotes'"

triple quotes(""" """) Eg, This is a paragraph. It is made up of multiple lines and sentences."""

2. Lists

List is an ordered sequence of items. Values in the list are called elements / items. It can be written as a list of comma-separated items (values) between square brackets[ ]. Items in the lists can be of different data types.Lists are just like the arrays, declared in other languages which is a ordered collection of data. It is very flexible as the items in a list do not need to be of the same type.

Creating List Lists in Python can be created by just placing the sequence inside the square brackets[].

The below example illustrates the creation of list in different ways:

Creating a List List = [] print("Initial blank List: ") print(List)

List = ['Pyhton Programming'] # Creating a List with the use of a String

print("\nList with the use of String: ") print(List) List = ["Python", "For", "Programming"] # Creating a List with the use of multiple values

print("\nList containing multiple values: ") print(List[0]) print(List[2]) The **output** for the above code is shown below:

Initial blank List:[] List with the use of String:['Pyhton Programming'] List containing multiple values:PyhtonProgramming

3. Tuple:

A tuple is same as list, except that the set of elements is enclosed in parentheses instead of square brackets. A tuple is an immutable list. i.e. once a tuple has been created, you can't add elements to a tuple or remove elements from the tuple.

Benefit of Tuple:

Tuples are faster than lists. If the user wants to protect the data from accidental changes, tuple can be used. Tuples can be used as keys in dictionaries, while lists can't.

4.Boolean

Data type with one of the two built-in values, True or False. Boolean objects that are equal to True are truthy (true), and those equal to False are falsy (false). But non-Boolean objects can be evaluated in Boolean context as well and determined to be true or false. It is denoted by the class bool.

5.Set

In Python, Set is an unordered collection of data type that is iterable, mutable and has no duplicate elements. The order of elements in a set is undefined though it may consist of various elements.Set items are unordered, unchangeable, and do not allow duplicate values.There are some properties for set data type:

1.Unordered-Unordered means that the items in a set do not have a defined order. Set items can appear in a different order every time you use them, and cannot be referred to by index or key.

2.Unchangeable-Set items are unchangeable, meaning that we cannot change the items after the set has been created. Once a set is created, you cannot change its items, but you can remove items and add new items. Duplicates Not Allowed Sets cannot have two items with the same value.

Creating Sets

Sets can be created by using the built-in set() function with an iterable object or a sequence by placing the sequence inside curly braces {}, separated by 'comma'. Type of elements in a set need not be the same, various mixed-up data type values can also be passed to the set.

Example:

set1 = set() print("Initial blank Set: ") print(set1)

Output: Initial blank Set: set()

6.Dictionary

Dictionary in Python is an unordered collection of data values, used to store data values like a map, which unlike other Data Types that hold only single value as an element, Dictionary holds key:value pair. Key-value is provided in the dictionary to make it more optimized. Each key-value pair in a Dictionary is separated by a colon :, whereas each key is separated by a 'comma'. Dictionary is created by using curly brackets. i,e. {}. Dictionary can also be created by the built-in function dict(). An empty dictionary can be created by just placing it to curly braces{}.

2.5 Variables

A variable allows us to store a value by assigning it to a name, which can be used later.They are Named memory locations to store values. Programmers generally choose names for their variables that are meaningful. It can be of any length. No space is allowed. We don't need to declare a variable before using it. In Python, we simply assign a value to a variable and it will exist.Python Variable is containers which store values. Python is not "statically typed". A variable is created the moment we first assign a value to it. A Python variable is a name given to a memory location. It is the basic unit of storage in a program.

2.5.1Rules for creating variables in Python

- A variable name must start with a letter or the underscore character.
- A variable name cannot start with a number.
- A variable name can only contain alpha-numeric characters and underscores (A-z, 0-9, and _).
- Variable names are case-sensitive (name, Name and NAME are three different variables).
- The reserved words(keywords) cannot be used naming the variable.

Declare the Variable

Let's see how to declare the variable and print the variable.

declaring the var

Number = 100 print(Number) Output: 100

2.5.2Global and Local Python Variables

Local variables are the ones that are defined and declared inside a function. We can not call this variable outside the function. Global variables are the ones that are defined and declared outside a function, and we need to use them inside a function.

Global keyword in Python

Global keyword is a keyword that allows a user to modify a variable outside of the current scope. It is used to create global variables from a non-global scope i.e inside a function. Global keyword is used inside a function only when we want to do assignments or when we want to change a variable.

Rules of global keyword:

- If a variable is assigned a value anywhere within the function's body, it's assumed to be a local unless explicitly declared as global.
- Variables that are only referenced inside a function are implicitly global.
- We Use global keyword to use a global variable inside a function.

- There is no need to use global keyword outside a function.

Example:

Python program to modify a global

x = 15 # value inside a function

def change(): global x # using a global keyword x = x + 5 # increment value of a by 5 print("Value of x inside a function :", x) change() print("Value of x outside a function :", x)

Output:

Value of x inside a function : 20 Value of x outside a function : 20

2.5.3 Object References

Let, we assign a variable x to value 5, and

x = 5 Another variable is y to the variable x. x = y

When Python looks at the first statement, what it does is that, first, it creates an object to represent the value 5. Then, it creates the variable x if it doesn't exist and made it a reference to this new object 5. The second line causes Python to create the variable y, and it is not assigned with x, rather it is made to reference that object that x does. The net effect is that the variables x and y wind up referencing the same object. This situation, with multiple names referencing the same object, is called a Shared Reference in Python.Now, if we write:

x = 'Good'

This statement makes a new object to represent 'Good' and makes x to reference this new object. Now if we assign the new value in Y, then the previous object refers to the garbage values.

y = "Computer"

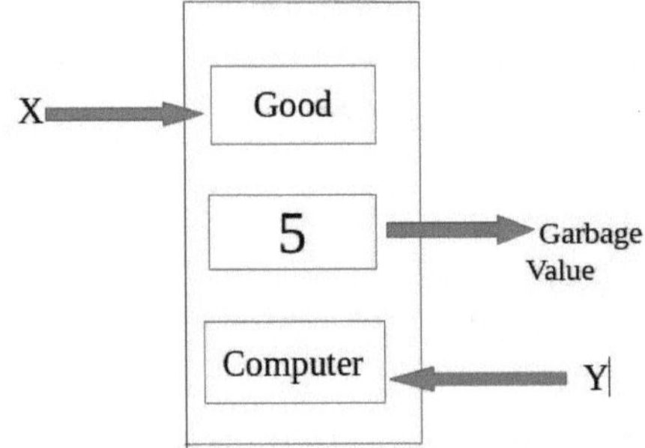

Fig-Object Reference

In this the references are allocated to variables in a machine for variables in pyhton programming.

Keywords

A keyword is a word that is reserved by a program because that word has a special meaning, typically a commands or parameters. Keywords are used in many different languages, but they all have similar functions and purposes. They help programmers write code more efficiently by allowing them to use words instead of having to spell out every single command. Keywords are sometimes called reserved names.Below is list of all the keywords which we use in python:

False	*class*	*finally*	*is*	*return*
None	*continue*	*for*	*lambda*	*try*
True	*def*	*from*	*nonlocal*	*while*
and	*del*	*global*	*not*	*with*
as	*elif*	*if*	*or*	*yield*
assert	*else*	*import*	*pass*	
break	*except*	*in*	*raise*	

Identifiers

Identifiers are the name given to variables, classes, methods, etc. For example, language = 'Python'Here, language is a variable (an identifier) which holds the value 'Python'.We cannot use keywords as variable names as they are reserved names that are built-in to Python.

Rules for Naming an Identifier

- Identifiers cannot be a keyword.
- Identifiers are case-sensitive.
- It can have a sequence of letters and digits. However, it must begin with a letter or _. The first letter of an identifier cannot be a digit.
- It's a convention to start an identifier with a letter rather _.
- Whitespaces are not allowed.
- We cannot use special symbols like !, @, #, $, and so on.

2.6 Statements

A statement is an instruction that the Python interpreter can execute. We have seen two kinds of statements: print and assignment. When you type a statement on the command line, Python executes it and displays the result, if there is one. The result of a print statement is a value. Assignment statements don't produce a result. A script usually contains a sequence of statements. If there is more than one statement, the results appear one at a time as the statements execute.

For example, the script

```
print( 1)
x = 2
print( x)
```

produces the output

```
1 2
```

Again, the assignment statement produces no output.

2.7 Expressions

A combination of operands and operators is called an expression. The expression in Python produces some value or result after being interpreted by the Python interpreter. An expression in Python is a combination of operators and operands. An example of expression can be : x=x+10. In this expression, the first 10 is added to the variable x. After the addition is performed, the result is assigned to the variable x.

2.7.1 Types of Expression in Python

We have various types of expression in Python, let us discuss them along with their respective examples.

1. Constant Expressions

A constant expression in Python that contains only constant values is known as a constant expression. In a constant expression in Python, the operator(s) is a constant. A constant is a value that cannot be changed after its initialization.

Example :

```
x = 10 + 15 # Here both 10 and 15 are constants but x is a variable.

print("The value of x is: ", x)
```

Output :

The value of x is: 25

2. Arithmetic Expressions

An expression in Python that contains a combination of operators, operands, and sometimes parenthesis is known as an arithmetic expression. The result of an arithmetic expression is also a numeric value just like the constant expression discussed above.

Example :

```
x = 10

y = 5

addition = x + y

subtraction = x - y

product = x * y

division = x / y

power = x**y
```

```
print("The sum of x and y is: ", addition)
print("The difference between x and y is: ", subtraction)
print("The product of x and y is: ", product)
print("The division of x and y is: ", division)
print("x to the power y is: ", power)
```

Output :

```
The sum of x and y is: 15
The difference between x and y is: 5
The product of x and y is: 50
The division of x and y is: 2.0
x to the power y is: 100000
```

3. Integral Expressions

An integral expression in Python is used for computations and type conversion (integer to float, a string to integer, etc.). An integral expression always produces an integer value as a resultant.

Example :

```
x = 10 # an integer number
y = 5.0 # a floating point number # we need to convert the floating-point number into an integer or vice versa for summation.
result = x + int(y)
print("The sum of x and y is: ", result)
```

Output :

```
The sum of x and y is: 15
```

4. Floating Expressions

A floating expression in Python is used for computations and type conversion (integer to float, a string to integer, etc.). A floating expression always produces a floating-point number as a resultant.

Example :

```
x = 10 # an integer number
```

```
y = 5.0 # a floating point number

# we need to convert the integer number into a floating-point number or vice versa for summation.

result = float(x) + y

print("The sum of x and y is: ", result)
```

Output :

The sum of x and y is: 15.0

5. Relational Expressions

A relational expression in Python can be considered as a combination of two or more arithmetic expressions joined using relational operators. The overall expression results in either True or False (boolean result). We have four types of relational operators in Python (i.e.>,<,>=,<=).

For example :

10+15>20

In this example, first, the arithmetic expressions (i.e. 10+15 and 20) are evaluated, and then the results are used for further comparison.

Example :

```
a = 25

b = 14

c = 48

d = 45 # The expression checks if the sum of (a and b) is the same as the difference of (c and d).

result = (a + b) == (c - d)

print("Type:", type(result))

print("The result of the expression is: ", result)
```

Output :

Type: <class ‘bool’>

The result of the expression is: False

6. Logical Expressions

As the name suggests, a logical expression performs the logical computation, and the overall expression results in either True or False (boolean result). We have three types of logical expressions in Python, let us discuss them briefly.

Example :

```
from operator import and
x = (10 == 9)
y = (7 > 5)
and_result = x and y
or_result = x or y
not_x = not x
print("The result of x and y is: ", and_result)
print("The result of x or y is: ", or_result)
print("The not of x is: ", not_x)
```

Output :

```
The result of x and y is: False
The result of x or y is: True
The not of x is: True
```

7. Bitwise Expressions

The expression in which the operation or computation is performed at the bit level is known as a bitwise expression in Python. The bitwise expression contains the bitwise operators.

Example :

```
x = 25
left_shift = x << 1
right_shift = x >> 1
print("One right shift of x results: ", right_shift)
print("One left shift of x results: ", left_shift)
```

Output :

```
One right shift of x results: 12
```

One left shift of x results: 50

8. Combinational Expressions

As the name suggests, a combination expression can contain a single or multiple expressions which result in an integer or boolean value depending upon the expressions involved.

Example :

x = 25 y = 35 result = x + (y << 1)

print("Result obtained : ", result)

Output :

Result obtained: 95

Whenever there are multiple expressions involved then the expressions are resolved based on their precedence or priority. Let us learn about the precedence of various operators in the following section.

Example:

x = 12 y = 14 z = 16 result_1 = x + y * z

print("Result of 'x + y + z' is: ", result_1)

result_2 = (x + y) * z print("Result of '(x + y) * z' is: ", result_2)

result_3 = x + (y * z) print("Result of 'x + (y * z)' is: ", result_3)

Output :

Result of 'x + y + z' is: 236 Result of '(x + y) * z' is: 416 Result of 'z + (y * z)' is: 236

2.8 Tuple Assignment

An assignment to all of the elements in a tuple using a single assignment statement. Python has a very powerful tuple assignment feature that allows a tuple of variables on the left of an assignment to be assigned values from a tuple on the right of the assignment. The left side is a tuple of variables; the right side is a tuple of values. Each value is assigned to its respective variable. All the expressions on the right side are evaluated before any of the assignments.

>>> (a, b, c, d) = (1, 2, 3)

ValueError: need more than 3 values to unpack

Example:

It is useful to swap the values of two variables. With conventional assignment statements, we have to use a temporary variable. For example, to swap a and b:

Tuple assignment solves the swap problem neatly:

(a, b) = (b, a)

One way to think of tuple assignment is as tuple packing/unpacking.

In tuple packing, the values on the left are 'packed' together in a tuple:

>>> b = ("George", 25, "20000") # tuple packing

In tuple unpacking, the values in a tuple on the right are 'unpacked' into the variables/names on the right:

>>> b = ("George", 25, "20000") # tuple packing >>> (name, age, salary) = b # tuple unpacking

>>>name 'George' >>>salary '20000'

2.9 Operators

Operators are the constructs which can manipulate the value of operands.Operators are the pillars of a program on which the logic is built in a specific programming language. Consider the expression 4 + 5 = 9. Here, 4 and 5 are called operands and + is called operator

Types of Operators:

-Python language supports the following types of operators

- Arithmetic Operators
- Comparison (Relational) Operators
- Assignment Operators
- Logical Operators
- Bitwise Operators
- Membership Operators
- Identity Operators

1.Arithmetic operators:

They are used to perform mathematical operations like addition, subtraction, multiplication etc.

Operator	Description	Example
+ Addition	Adds values on either side of the operator.	a + b = 30
- Subtraction	Subtracts right hand operand from left hand operand.	a – b = -10
* Multiplication	Multiplies values on either side of the operator	a * b = 200
/ Division	Divides left hand operand by right hand operand	b / a = 2
% Modulus	Divides left hand operand by right hand operand and returns remainder	b % a = 0
** Exponent	Performs exponential (power) calculation on operators	a**b =10 to the power 20
//	Floor Division - The division of operands where the result is the quotient in which the digits after the decimal point are removed	5//2=2

Table-Arithmetic Operators and their functionalities

2.Comparison (Relational) Operators:

Comparison operators are used to compare values.It either returns True or False according to the condition .Comparison Operators In Python compares the values on either side of the operand and determines the relation between them. It is also referred to as relational operators. Various comparison operators in python are (==, != , <>, >,<=, etc.).

Operator	Description	Example
==	If the values of two operands are equal, then the condition	(a == b) is
	becomes true.	not true.
!=	If values of two operands are not equal, then condition becomes true.	(a!=b) is true
>	If the value of left operand is greater than the value of right operand, then condition becomes true.	(a > b) is not true.
<	If the value of left operand is less than the value of right operand, then condition becomes true.	(a < b) is true.
>=	If the value of left operand is greater than or equal to the value of right operand, then condition becomes true.	(a >= b) is not true.
<=	If the value of left operand is less than or equal to the value of right operand, then condition becomes true.	(a <= b) is true.

Table-Comparision Operators and their functionalities

3.Assignment Operators:

Assignment operators are used in Python to assign values to variables.Assignment Operators in Python are used for assigning the value of the right operand to the left operand. Various assignment operators used in Python are (+=, – = , *=, /= , etc.).

Operator	Description	Example
=	Assigns values from right side operands to left side operand	c = a + b assigns value of a + b into c
+= Add AND	It adds right operand to the left operand and assign the result to left operand	c += a is equivalent to c = c + a
-= Subtract AND	It subtracts right operand from the left operand and assign the result to left operand	c -= a is equivalent to c = c - a
*= Multiply AND	It multiplies right operand with the left operand and assign the result to left operand	c *= a is equivalent to c = c * a
/= Divide AND	It divides left operand with the right operand and assign the result to left operand	c /= a is equivalent to c = c / ac /= a is equivalent to c = c / a
%= Modulus AND	It takes modulus using two operands and assign the result to left operand	c %= a is equivalent to c = c % a
**= Exponent AND	Performs exponential (power) calculation on operators and assign value to the left operand	c **= a is equivalent to c = c ** a
//= Floor Division	It performs floor division on operators and assign value to the left operand	c //= a is equivalent to c = c // a

Table-Assignment Operators and their functionalities

4.Logical Operators:

Logical operators are the and, or, not operators. Logical operators in Python are used for conditional statements are true or false. Logical operators in Python are AND, OR and NOT. For logical operators following condition are applied.

Operator	Meaning	Example
and	True if both the operands are true	x and y
or	True if either of the operands is true	x or y
not	True if operand is false (complements the operand)	not x

Table-Logical Operators and their functionalities

5.Bitwise Operators:

A bitwise operation operates on one or more bit patterns at the level of individual Bits. Bitwise operations are processes that engage with individual bits, which are the fundamental constituent of any sort of data in a computer. A binary value of 0 or 1 is assigned to each bit.

Operator	Meaning	Example
&	Bitwise AND	x& y = 0 (0000 0000)
|	Bitwise OR	x | y = 14 (0000 1110)
~	Bitwise NOT	~x = -11 (1111 0101)
^	Bitwise XOR	x ^ y = 14 (0000 1110)
>>	Bitwise right shift	x>> 2 = 2 (0000 0010)
<<	Bitwise left shift	x<< 2 = 40 (0010 1000)

Table-Bit-wise Operators and their functionalities

6.Membership Operators:

Evaluates to find a value or a variable is in the specified sequence of string, list, tuple, dictionary or not.

Operator	Meaning	Example
in	True if value/variable is found in the sequence	5 in x
not in	True if value/variable is not found in the sequence	5 not in x

Table-Membership Operators and their functionalities

7.Identity Operators

They are used to check if two values (or variables) are located on the same part of the memory.

Operator	Meaning	Example
is	True if the operands are identical (refer to the same object)	x is True
is not	True if the operands are not identical (do not refer to the same object)	x is not True

Table-Identity Operators and their functionalities

2.9.1 Operator Precedence

When an expression contains more than one operator, the order of evaluation depends on the order of operations. For mathematical operators, Python follows mathematical convention. The acronym PEMDAS (Parentheses, Exponentiation, Multiplication, Division, Addition, Subtraction) is a useful way to remember the rules:

- Parentheses have the highest precedence and can be used to force an expression to evaluate in the order you want. Since expressions in parentheses are evaluated first, 2 * (3-1)is 4, and (1+1)**(5-2) is 8.
- You can also use parentheses to make an expression easier to read, as in (minute * 100) / 60, even if it doesn't change the result.
- Exponentiation has the next highest precedence, so 1 + 2**3 is 9, not 27, and 2 *3**2 is 18, not 36.
- Multiplication and Division have higher precedence than Addition and Subtraction. So 2*3-1 is 5, not 4, and 6+4/2 is 8, not 5.
- Operators with the same precedence are evaluated from left to right (except exponentiation).

Operator	Description
**	Exponentiation (raise to the power)
~ + -	Complement, unary plus and minus (method names for the last two are +@ and -@)
* / % //	Multiply, divide, modulo and floor division
+ -	Addition and subtraction
>> <<	Right and left bitwise shift
&	Bitwise 'AND'
^ |	Bitwise exclusive `OR' and regular `OR'
<= < > >=	Comparison operators
<> == !=	Equality operators
= %= /= //= -= += *= **=	Assignment operators
is is not	Identity operators
in not in	Membership operators
not or and	Logical operators

Table-Operator Precedence

In the above table the priority is first given to that variable that occurs first in the above table. The operator precedence determines which operators need to be evaluated first. To avoid ambiguity in values, precedence operators are necessary. Just like in normal multiplication method, multiplication has a higher precedence than addition. For example in 3+ 4*5, the answer is 23, to change the order of precedence we use a parentheses (3+4)*5, now the answer is 35. Precedence operator used in Python are (unary + – ~, **, * / %, + – , &) etc.

2.10 Comments

Comments in Python is the inclusion of short descriptions along with the code to increase its readability. A developer uses them to write his or her thought process while writing the code. It explains the basic logic behind why a particular line of code was written. They are just meant for the coders themselves or other developers to understand a piece of code, especially since the Python interpreter completely ignores comments in Python.Comments in Python are identified with a **hash** symbol, #, and extend to the end of the line. Hash characters in a string are not considered comments, however. There are three ways to write a comment - as a separate line, beside the corresponding statement of code, or as a multi-line comment block.

There are multiple uses of writing comments in Python. Some significant uses include:

- Increasing readability
- Explaining the code to others
- Understanding the code easily after a long-term
- Including resources
- Re-using the existing code

Comments in Python provide numerous advantages. Their primary benefits include:

- Makes the code easily understandable by other programmers
- The code becomes self-explanatory
- Helps remember why we used a specific command, method, or function in the code
- Enables the interpreter to ignore some part of the code while testing

LINES AND INDENTATION:

Most of the programming languages like C, C++, Java use braces { } to define a block of code. But, python uses indentation. Blocks of code are denoted by line indentation. It is a space given to the block of codes for class and function definitions or flow control.

2.10.1 Different Types of Comments:

1.Single-Line Comments

Single-line comments begin with the "#" character. Anything that is written in a single line after '#' is considered as a comment. The syntax for writing single-line comments is:

 # comments here

2.Multi-Line Comments

Python does not support multi-line comments. However, there are multiple ways to overcome this issue. None of these ways are technically multi-line comments, but you can use them as one. The first way is by using # at the beginning of each line of the comment.

Example:

#You can use

#the symbol for every

#new line

The next way is by using string literals but not assigning them to any variables. If you do not assign a string literal to a variable, the Python interpreter ignores it. Use this to your advantage to write multi-line comments. You can either use a single ('') quotation or double ("") quotation.

Example:
a='Hello Everybody'

'this a string which is not assigned to any variable'.

You can also use multi-line strings for commenting. To do this, use either a '' or "" quotation marks three times.

Example:

''' In this way we write a multiple line string in python programming

'''

Python Docstrings

Python provides an in-built feature called docstrings for commenting on modules, methods, functions, objects, and classes. They are written in the first line after defining a module, function, method, etc., using three quotation marks ('' or ""). If you do not use it in the first line, the interpreter will not take it as a docstring. You can also access docstrings using the __doc__ attribute.

2.10.2 Writing Good Comments

Comments are a crucial part of a program. Hence, it is essential to learn how to write good comments. Here are some characteristics that define good comments.

- Ensure that they are concise
- Don't write generic comments; only have them if they add information

(a=10 #assigning 10 to a, avoid writing such generic comments)

- Write comments that describe the overall task of a function or method and not specific details
- Good comments are self-explanatory ,Don't write redundant comments

2.11 Input and Output

INPUT:

Input is data entered by user (end user) in the program. In python, **input () function** is available for input.A function is defined as a block of organized, reusable code used to perform a single, related action. In Python 2, you have a built-in function raw_input(), whereas in Python 3, you have input(). The program will resume once the user presses the ENTER or RETURN key.To capture the input in your program, you will need a variable.

Syntax for input() is:

variable = input ("data")

Example:

>>>x=input("enter the name:") enter the name: george >>>y=int(input("enter the number"))

enter the number 3

Give a helpful hint during the prompt

It is often a good idea to tell the user what to input. You can do this by putting the hint in quotes inside the input parentheses. The hint will come in the next line and will wait for the user input. You can then type the input and when you hit the ENTER key, it will capture the input. In this example, "tell me a beautiful number" is the hint. This gets printed in the next line when asking for the input. If you type 6, this will be assigned to the variable beautiful_number which we can print later.

>>> beautiful_number = input("tell me a beautiful number ") tell me a beautiful number 6

>>> print(beautiful_number) '6'

OUTPUT:

Output can be displayed to the user using Print statement . To output your data to the screen, use the print() function. You can write print(argument) and this will print the argument in the next line when you press the ENTER key. Definitions to remember: An argument is a value you pass to a function when calling it. A value is a letter or a number. A variable is a name that refers to a value. It begins with a letter. An assignment statement creates new variables and gives them values.

Syntax:

print (expression/constant/variable)

Example:

print ("Hello") Hello

Say you want to print a specific string (a sequence of characters such as letters, punctuation marks, numbers, and letters) N number of times. The (asterisk) * operator performs repetition on strings. You can print "5" six times.

>>> print("5"*6) 555555

You can separate the output using the comma delimiter. By default, this adds a space between the output items. For example, the sequence of numbers 5,6,7 separated by comma , gets printed with a space between one number and the next.

>>> print(5,6,7) 5 6 7

To change the output to what you want, use the keyword arguments sep and end to print ( ). When separating the output with a comma delimiter, you can also define the separation format using the sep keyword.

>>> print('LOVE', 30, 82.2) LOVE 30 82.2

>>> print('LOVE', 30, 82.2, sep=',') 'LOVE', 30, 82.2

By default, print goes to a new line at the end. You can change this by using the keyword end as shown in the example below.

>>> print('LOVE', 30, 82.2, sep=',', end='!!\n') 'LOVE', 30, 82.2!!

For example, you can print the letters in the word "python" and all the letters will come in a new line.

>>> for i in "python": print(i) p y t h o n

You can change this default implementation. You can have a colon : between the letters instead of a new line.

>>> for i in "python": print(i, end=":") p:y:t:h:o:n:

2.12 Problems to Solve

1. Exchange the values of two variables

Code:

x = 5 y = 10 print('Before swapping:') print (x) print (y) temp = x x = y y = temp print('After swapping:') print (x) print (y)

Output:

Before swapping: 5 10
After swapping: 10 5

2. Circulate the values of n variables

def rotate(l,order): for i in range(0,order): j=len(l)-1 while j>0: temp=l[j] l[j]=l[j-1] l[j-1]=temp j=j-1 print (i,'rotation',l) return l=[1,2,3,4,5] rotate(l,3)

Output: 0 rotation [5, 1, 2, 3, 4] 1 rotation [4, 5, 1, 2, 3] 2 rotation [3, 4, 5, 1, 2]

3. Distance between two points

import math def distance(x1,y1,x2,y2): dx=x2-x1 dy=y2-y1 print("The value of dx is", dx) print("The value of dy is", dy) d= (dx**2 + dy**2) dist=math.sqrt(d) return dist x1 = float(input("Enter the first Number: ")) x2 = float(input("Enter the Second Number: ")) y1 = float(input("Enter the third number: ")) y2 = float(input("Enter the forth number: ")) z=distance(x1,x2,y1,y2) print("The distance between two points are", z)

Output: Enter the first Number: 2 Enter the Second Number: 4
Enter the third number: 6 Enter the forth number: 12
The value of dx is 4.0 The value of dy is 8.0 The distance between two points are 8.9442719099

CHAPTER THREE

CONTROL FLOW, FUNCTIONS, STRINGS

Introduction

There comes situations in real life when we need to make some decisions and based on these decisions, we decide what should we do next. Similar situations arise in programming also where we need to make some decisions and based on these decisions we will execute the next block of code. Decision-making statements in programming languages decide the direction of the flow of program execution. So in sequential statements we have two different types in it. One is Conditional Statements and the other one is Iterative Statements. Conditional Statements are the statements where the flow of control moves forward only when it is true. Then what about flow of control when it is false? In such cases it either skips the conditional loop or alternative statements will be provided. In iterative case we repeat a set of statements if the condition is true or else it just skips the loop. In case if we want to repeat some statements with more iterations then we use Functions. Functions are considered as good programming style as it helps in reusing of code. Strings are used to represent the series of characters. Python provides many functions to access the strings easily. Strings are also used for writing comments and used in may more applications.

3.1 Conditionals

Conditional statements help you to make a decision based on certain conditions. These conditions are specified by a set of conditional statements having boolean expressions which are evaluated to a boolean value of true or false.

3.1.1 Boolean values and operators

Boolean Data Type

Programming uses a number of different data types. The data type of an object determines what type of values an object can have and what operations can be performed on the object. Commonly used data types include strings, numbers, lists and arrays. This lesson will look more closely at one data type that is widely used: Boolean data. The Boolean data type can only represent two values: true or false. Typically, a 1 is used to represent true, and a 0 is used to represent false. Boolean data is widely used when working with conditions.

Boolean Expression

Boolean data are used in **Boolean expressions**, which are expressions in a programming language that produce a Boolean value. An expression in programming is any combination of values, variables and operators that produce a new value. For example, 2 + 3 is an expression, and the result is the new value 5. When you use a Boolean expression, the only logical result can be true or false. Consider the following example where a user inputs two values, and a computer program determines whether the first one is smaller than the second one or not.

$X = 8\ y = 7\ x < \mathrm{y}$

In this example, the part '$x < y$' is the Boolean expression. You are asking whether x is less than y, and the answer can only be a yes or a no - which means true or false in programming.The Boolean type is the primary result of conditional statements, which are used to control workflow in program. For example, if a particular condition is true, then do this; if the condition is false, then do something else.

There are two main types of Boolean operators in Python.

- **Comparison Operators:** Python comparison operators compare two values of the same type and return a Boolean value of True or False.
- **Logical Operators:** Python logical operators combine the results of other expressions and return True or False.

In addition to the comparison and logical operators, Python has a bool type. Any variable assigned the value of True or False has a type of bool. It is possible to confirm the type of a variable using the built-in type function. The Python bool function lets programmers evaluate any variable, expression, or object as a Boolean value. This function always returns True or False. Python uses its own set of rules to determine the truth value of a variable. Some of the less obvious rules guiding whether something is True or False are included in the list below.

- A positive or negative integer or real number of any size is always True. The values 0 and 0.0 are False.Rounding errors resulting from mathematical operations on real numbers can cause confusing or misleading results. Even if the variable “should” be zero, rounding operations could mean it holds a very small non-zero value. This would evaluate as True

1.Comparison Operators in Python

Python comparison operators compare two items, but they can only be used on items that are comparable. For instance, two integers can be compared for equality, as can two strings. But two items with different types, such as an integer and a string, cannot be compared. If such comparisons are attempted, an error similar to TypeError: ‘<’ not supported between instances of ‘int’ and ’str' is returned. The items being compared can be either constants or variables.

There are several different comparison operators, which typically return Boolean values. Not all operators make sense for all types. The most common of these operators include:

- ==: The “equal to” operator. !=: The “not equal to” operator. <: The “less than” operator. >: The “greater than” operator. <=: The “less than or equal to” operator. >=: The “greater than or equal to” operator.

Some of these operators are mirror images to one another and some are a convenient shorthand for an operation that would otherwise require two comparisons.

2.Logical Operators in Python

Python’s logical operators are used to evaluate Boolean expressions. They perform simple Boolean arithmetic on one or two inputs and return either True or False. Logical operators can be chained together to form even longer expressions. The logic of each operator can be demonstrated using a *Truth Table*. The truth table for a given operation lists the output for each possible combination of inputs. It is used to analyze Boolean functions in an easy-to-understand format. Boolean expressions can be created in Python from the three main logical operators.

- and: This is the Python “logical and” operator. It returns True if both expressions are True and False otherwise. or: The Python “logical or” operator returns True if either expression is True and False otherwise. not: Python’s “logical not” operator returns True only if the expression it is evaluating is False.

3.1.2 Conditional Statements

Conditional Statement in Python perform different computations or actions depending on whether a specific Boolean constraint evaluates to true or false. The following are the conditional statements provided by Python.

- if if..else Nested if if-elif statements.

1. IF Statement

The If statement is the most fundamental decision-making statement, in which the code is executed based on whether it meets the specified condition. It has a code body that only executes if the condition in the if statement is true. The statement can be a single line or a block of code.The if statement is used to test a particular condition and if the condition is true, it executes a block of code known as if-block. The condition of if statement can be any valid logical expression which can be either evaluated to true or false. The flow chart is drawn as shown below:

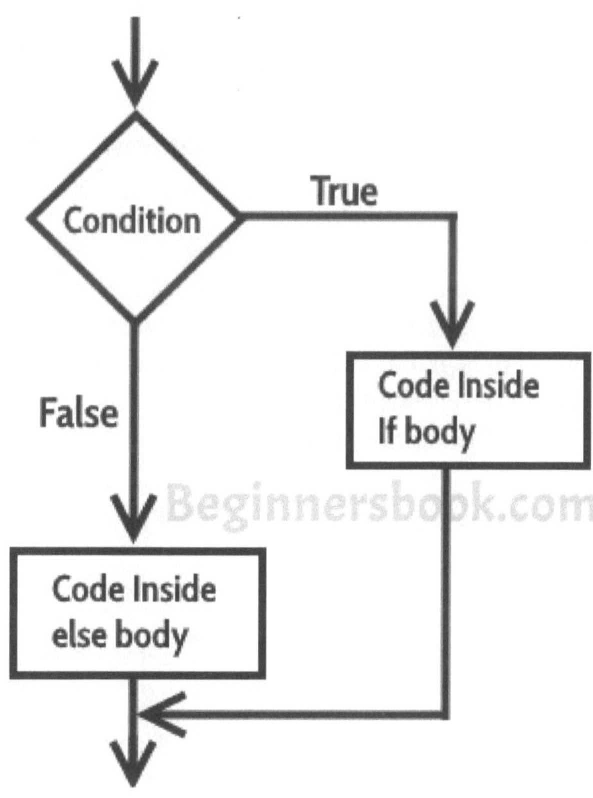

Fig-Flow Chart of If statement

The if statement in Python has the subsequent syntax:

if expression:

Statement

NOTE: The identation is important in writing conditional statements as we differentiate other statements with those of conditional statements. The identation indicates the start of a block.

Example 1 : Program to print the largest of the three numbers.

a=int(input("Enter a? ")) b=int(input("Enter b? ")) c=int(input("Enter c? "))

if a>b and a>c: print("a is largest")

if b>a and b>c: print("b is largest")

if c>a and c>b: print("c is largest");

Output:

Enter a? 100 Enter b? 120 Enter c? 130 c is largest

2.The if-else statement

The if-else statement provides an else block combined with the if statement which is executed in the false case of the condition. If the condition is true, then the if-block is executed. Otherwise, the else-block is executed. First, the test expression is checked. If it is true, the statements present in the body of the if block will execute. Next, the statements present below the if block is executed. In case the test expression has false results, the statements present in the else body are executed, and then the statements below the if-else are executed.Below is the entire workflow of how the if-else statement works.

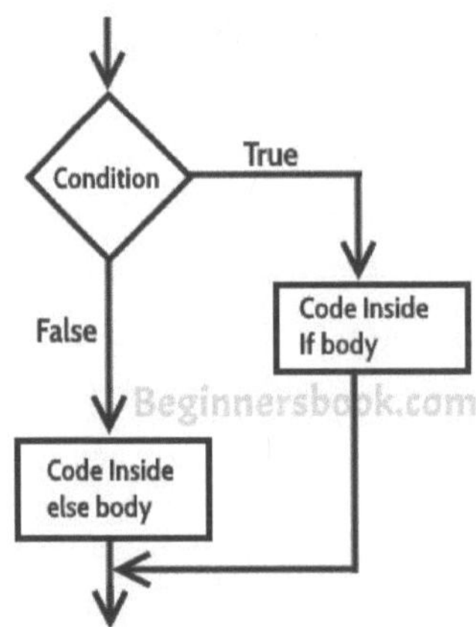

Fig- Flow Chart representation of if-else statements

The if statement in Python has the subsequent **syntax:**

if(condition): Statements

else:Statements

Example 1: Program to check whether a number is even or not.

num = int(input("enter the number?")) if num%2 == 0: print("Number is even...")

else: print("Number is odd...")

Output: enter the number?10 Number is even

3.The if-elif statement

The elif statement enables us to check multiple conditions and execute the specific block of statements depending upon the true condition among them. We can have any number of elif statements in our program depending upon our need.

The **syntax** of the elif statement is given below.

If expression1: # block of statements

elif expression 2: # block of statements

elif expression 3: # block of statements

else: # block of statements

The flow chart for if-elif statements is given as shown below

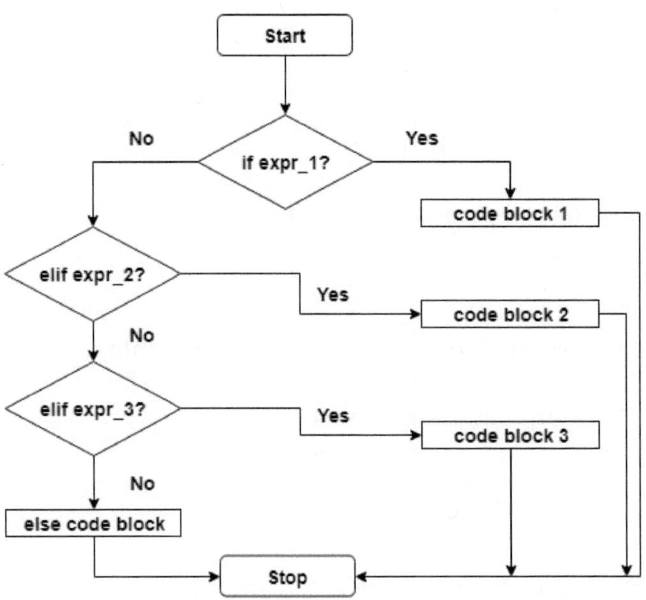

Fig- Flow chart for if-elif statements.

Example 1

```
marks= int(input("Enter the marks? "))

if marks > 85 and marks <=100: print("Congrats ! You scored grade A ...")

elif marks > 60 and marks <= 85: print("You scored grade B + ...")

elif marks>40 and marks<=60: print("You scored grade B ...")

elif (marks>30 and marks<=40): print("You scored grade C...")

else: print("Sorry you have failed")
```

Output:

Enter the marks ? 90 Congrats ! You scored grade A ...

4.Nested if

When an if a statement is present inside another if statement, it is called a nested IF statement. This situation occurs when you have to filter a variable multiple times.In nested IF statements, you should always take care of the indentation to define the scope of each statement.

The workflow below demonstrates how nested IF statements work:

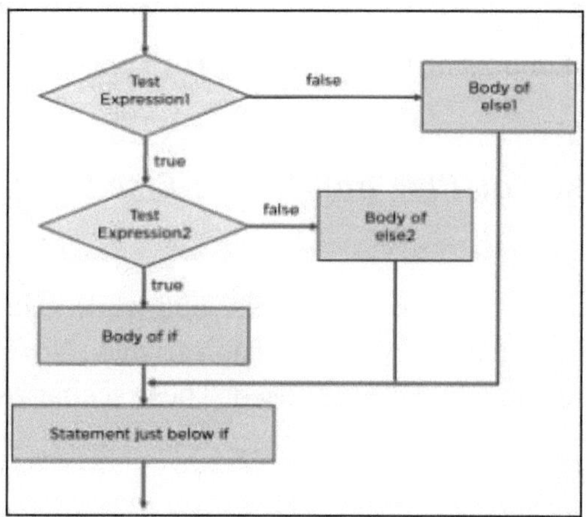

Fig-Flow Chart of Nested If statement

Syntax:

if (condition1): #Executes if condition1 is true

if (condition2): #Executes if condition2 is true

#Condition2 ends here #Condition1 ends here

Example -1: Finding a number whether it is zero/positive/negative

num = 15 if num >= 0: if num == 0: print("Zero")

else: print("Positive number") else: print("Negative number")

Output: *Positive number*

3.1.3 Iteration

Iteration statements or loop statements allow us to execute a block of statements as long as the condition is true. Loops statements are used when we need to run same code again and again, each time with a different value.For example, if we want to show a message **100** times, then we can use a loop. It's just a simple example; you can achieve much more with loops. Python provides three ways for executing the loops. While all the ways provide similar basic functionality, they differ in their syntax and condition checking time.

Type of Iteration Statements In Python 3

In Python Iteration (Loops) statements are of three types :-

1.While Loop 2.For Loop 3.Nested For Loops

Scenarios to use For Else and While Else in Python

It is not mandatory or necessary that we must use the for-else and while-else features in our Python programs We can do an alternate implementation by using a flag variable.. Now, we are going to see three such scenarios where for else and while else are used. These scenarios are as follows:

To be used in a searching program To check the limits To handle exceptions

1. While Loop In Python

While Loop In Python is used to execute a block of statement as long as a given condition is true. And when the condition is false, the control will come out of the loop. The condition is checked every time at the beginning of the loop. The given condition, i.e., conditional_expression, is evaluated initially in the Python while loop. Then, if the conditional expression gives a boolean value True, the while loop statements are executed. The conditional expression is verified again when the complete code block is executed. This procedure repeatedly occurs until the conditional expression returns the boolean value False.

- The statements of the Python while loop are dictated by indentation.
- The code block begins when a statement is indented & ends with the very first unindented statement.
- Any non-zero number in Python is interpreted as boolean True. False is interpreted as None and 0.

While Loop Syntax

while (condition): statements

Example Of While Loop

x = 0 while (x < 5): print(x) x = x + 1

Output :-0 1 2 3 4

While Loop With Else In Python

The else part is executed if the condition in the while loop becomes False. Python supports to have an else statement associated with a loop statement.

Syntax of While Loop With Else

while (condition): loop statements else: else statements

Example of While Loop With Else

x = 1 while (x < 5): print('inside while loop value of x is ',x)
x = x + 1 else: print('inside else value of x is ', x)

***Output** :- inside while loop value of x is 1 inside while loop value of x is 2 inside while loop value of x is 3 inside while loop value of x is 4 inside else value of x is 5*

Infinite While Loop In Python

A Infinite loop is a loop in which condition always remain True. A loop becomes infinite loop if a condition never becomes FALSE. You must use caution when using while loops because of the possibility that this condition never resolves to a FALSE value. This results in a loop that never ends. Such a loop is called an infinite loop.

Example of Infinite While Loop

x = 1 while (x == 1): print('hello')

Output :- hello hello hello

2. For Loop In Python

For loop in Python is used to iterate over items of any sequence, such as a list or a string. In Python, the for loop is often used to iterate over iterable objects such as lists, tuples, or strings. The for-loop is usually used on an iterable object such as a list or the in-built range function. The for statement in Python traverses through the elements of a series, running the block of code each time. The for statement is in opposition to the "while" loop, which is employed whenever a condition requires to be verified each repetition or when a piece of code is to be repeated indefinitely.

For Loop Syntax

for val in sequence:

statements

Example of For Loop

```
for i in range(1,5): print(i)
```

Output :- 1 2 3 4

The range() Function In Python

The range() function is a built-in that is used to iterate over a sequence of numbers. Because the "range" function appears so frequently in for loops, we might mistakenly believe the range is a component of the syntax of for loop. It isn't: it's a Python built-in method that provides a series that follows a specified pattern (usually serial integers), fulfilling the criteria of giving a series for the for expression to run over.

Syntax Of range() Function

```
range(start, stop[, step])
```

The range() Function Parameters

start: Starting number of the sequence.
stop: Generate numbers up to, but not including this number.
step(Optional): Determines the increment between each numbers in the sequence.

Example 1 of range() function using step parameter

```
for i in range(2,9,2):
print(i)
```

Output :- 2 4 6 8

Example 2 of range() function

```
for i in range(0,-10,-2): print(i)
```

Output :- 0 -2 -4 -6 -8

For Loop With Else In Python

The else is an optional block that can be used with for loop.The else block with for loop executed only if for loops terminates normally.This means that the loop did not encounter any break. Python allows you to connect an else expression with a loop expression.

Example of For Loop With Else

list=[2,3,4,6,7] for i in range(0,len(list)): if(list[i]==5): print('list has 5') break else: print('list does not have 5')

Output :-list does not have 5

3.1.4 Break

'Break' in Python is a loop control statement. It is used to control the sequence of the loop. Suppose you want to terminate a loop and skip to the next code after the loop; break will help you do that. A typical scenario of using the Break in Python is when an external condition triggers the loop's termination.Another use case for using 'Break' in Python is when you've taken an input for something, printed it using a loop, and want to give the user an option to print it again. If the user inputs "No," you can terminate the loop.

Syntax of Break in Python

break

It is used after the loop statements.

Flowchart of Break in Python

The following flowchart shows the use and control flow of a break statement in a loop.

3.1.5 Continue

In Python, loops repeat processes on their own in an efficient way. However, there might be occasions when we wish to leave the current loop entirely, skip iteration, or dismiss the condition controlling the loop. We use Loop control statements in such cases. The continue keyword is a loop control statement that allows us to change the loop's control. In Python, the continue keyword return control of the iteration to the beginning of the Python for loop or Python while loop.

Code

for iterator in range(10,21):

If iterator is equals to 15, loop will continue to the next iteration

if iterator ==15: continue print(iterator)
otherwise printing the value of iterator print(iterator)

Output:

10 11 12 13 14 16 17 18 19 20

3.1.6 Pass

The null statement is another name for the pass statement. A Comment is not ignored by the Python interpreter, whereas a pass statement is not. Hence, they two are different Python keywords. We can use the pass statement as a placeholder when unsure what code to provide. So, we only have to place the pass on that line. Pass may be used when we don't wish any code to be executed.

Syntax of the Pass Keyword

Keyword:

pass

Example of the Pass Statement

Code

sequence ={"Python","Pass","Statement","Placeholder"}

for value in sequence:

if value =="Pass": pass # leaving an empty if block using the pass keyword

else: print("Not reached pass keyword: ",value)

Output:

Not reached pass keyword: Python Not reached pass keyword: Placeholder Not reached pass keyword:

3.2 Functions

A function is a block of organized, reusable code that is used to perform a single, related action. Functions provide better modularity for your application and a high degree of code reusing. As you already know, Python gives you many built-in functions like print(), etc. but you can also create your own functions. These functions are called *user-defined functions.*So to write a function we do follow some steps. Those steps are described as below.

1. Defining a Function
2. Calling a Functions

1.Defining a Function

You can define functions to provide the required functionality. Here are simple rules to define a function in Python.

- Function blocks begin with the keyword **def** followed by the function name and parentheses (( )).
- Any input parameters or arguments should be placed within these parentheses. You can also define parameters inside these parentheses.
- The first statement of a function can be an optional statement - the documentation string of the function or *docstring.*
- The code block within every function starts with a colon (:) and is indented.
- The statement return [expression] exits a function, optionally passing back an expression to the caller. A return statement with no arguments is the same as return None.

Syntax

def functionname(parameters): function_suite #Statements return [expression]

By default, parameters have a positional behavior and you need to inform them in the same order that they were defined.

Example

The following function takes a string as input parameter and prints it on standard screen.

Code:

def printme(str): "This prints a passed string into this function" print str

return

2.Calling a Function

Defining a function only gives it a name, specifies the parameters that are to be included in the function and structures the blocks of code. Once the basic structure of a function is finalized, you can execute it by calling it from another function or directly from the Python prompt. The basic syntax for calling a function is given as follow:

function_name(arg1, arg2, ..., argN)

Following is the example to call printme() function

Example:

Function definition is here

def printme(str): "This prints a passed string into this function"

print str return;

Now you can call printme function

printme("I'm first call to user defined function!") printme("Again second call to the same function")

When the above code is executed, it produces the following result –

Output:

I'm first call to user defined function! Again second call to the same function Basically we call a function in two ways :

1.Pass by Reference

2. Pass by Value

3.2.1 Return Statement:

The **Python** return **statement** is a special statement that you can use inside a function or method to send the function's result back to the caller. A return statement consists of the return keyword followed by an optional **return value**. The return value of a Python function can be any Python object. Everything in Python is an object. So, your functions can return numeric values (int, float, and complex values), collections and sequences of objects (list, tuple, dictionary, or set objects), user-defined objects, classes, functions, and even modules or packages.

1.Explicit return Statements

An **explicit** return **statement** immediately terminates a function execution and sends the return value back to the caller code. To add an explicit return statement to a Python function, you need to use return followed by an optional return value:

>>> def return_42(): return 42

An explicit return statement ...

>>> return_42() # The caller code gets 42 42

When you define return_42(), you add an explicit return statement (return 42) at the end of the function's code block. 42 is the explicit return value of return_42(). This means that any time you call return_42(), the function will send 42 back to the caller.

If you define a function with an explicit return statement that has an explicit return value, then you can use that return value in any expression:

>>> num = return_42() >>> num 42 >>> return_42() * 2 84 >>> return_42() + 5 47

Since return_42() returns a numeric value, you can use that value in a math expression or any other kind of expression in which the value has a logical or coherent meaning. This is how a caller code can take advantage of a function's return value. Note that you can use a return statement only inside a function or method definition. If you use it anywhere else, then you'll get a SyntaxError:

>>> return 42 File "<stdin>", line 1 SyntaxError: 'return' outside function

When you use return outside a function or method, you get a SyntaxError telling you that the statement can't be used outside a function.

2.Implicit return Statements

A Python function will always have a return value. There is no notion of procedure or routine in Python. So, if you don't explicitly use a return value in a return statement, or if you totally omit the return statement, then Python will implicitly return a default value for you. That default return value will always be None. Say you're writing a function that adds 1 to a number x, but you forget to supply a return statement. In this case, you'll get an **implicit** return **statement** that uses None as a return value:

>>> def add_one(x): # No return statement at all result = x + 1 >>> value = add_one(5) >>> value>>> print(value) None

If you don't supply an explicit return statement with an explicit return value, then Python will supply an implicit return statement using None as a return value. In the above example, add_one() adds 1 to x and stores the value in result but it doesn't return result. That's why you get value = None instead of value = 6. To fix the problem, you need to either return result or directly return x + 1.

3.2.3 Function Arguments

When we define and call a Python function, the term parameter and argument is used to pass information to the function.

- **parameter:** It is the variable listed inside the parentheses in the function definition.
- **argument:** It is a value sent to the function when it is called. It is data on which function performs some action and returns the result.

It is not mandatory to use arguments in function definition. But if you need to process user data, you need arguments in the function definition to accept that data. Also, we use argument in function definition when we need to perform the same task multiple times with different data. If the function is defined with parameters, the arguments passed must match one of the arguments the function accepts when calling.

You can call a function by using the following types of formal arguments –

- Default argument
- Keyword arguments (named arguments)
- Positional arguments
- Arbitrary arguments (variable-length arguments *args and **kwargs)

1.Default Argument

In a function, arguments can have default values. We assign default values to the argument using the '=' (assignment) operator at the time of function definition. You can define a function with any number of default arguments. The default value of an argument will be used inside a function if we do not pass a value to that argument at the time of the function call. Due to this, the default arguments become optional during the function call. It overrides the default value if we provide a value to the default arguments during function calls.

Example:

Let's define a function student() with four arguments name, age, grade, and school. In this function, grade and school are default arguments with default values.

- If you call a function without school and grade arguments, then the default values of grade and school are used. The age and name parameters do not have default values and are required (mandatory) during a function call.

function with 2 keyword arguments grade and school

def student(name, age, grade="Five", school="ABC School"):

print('Student Details:', name, age, grade, school)

without passing grade and school # Passing only the mandatory arguments student('Jon', 12) # Output: Student Details: Jon 12 Five ABC School

Passing one of the default arguments:

If you pass values of the grade and school arguments while calling a function, then those values are used instead of default values.

Example:

def student(name, age, grade="Five", school="ABC School"):

print('Student Details:', name, age, grade, school)

not passing a school value (default value is used) # six is assigned to grade student('Kelly', 12, 'Six') # passign all arguments student('Jessa', 12, 'Seven', 'XYZ School')

Output: Student Details: Kelly 12 Six ABC School Student Details: Jessa 12 Seven XYZ School

2. Keyword Arguments

Usually, at the time of the function call, values get assigned to the arguments according to their position. So we must pass values in the same sequence defined in a function definition. . Keyword arguments are those arguments where **values get assigned to the arguments by their keyword (name)** when the function is called. It is preceded by the variable name and an (=) assignment operator. The Keyword Argument is also called a named argument.

Example:

function with 2 keyword arguments def student(name, age): print('Student Details:', name, age)

default function call student('Jessa', 14) # both keyword arguments student(name='Jon', age=12) # 1 positional and 1 keyword student('Donald', age=13)

Output: Student Details: Jessa 14 Student Details: Jon 12 Student Details: Donald 13

Change the sequence of keyword arguments

Also, you can change the sequence of keyword arguments by using their name in function calls. Python allows functions to be called using keyword arguments. But all the keyword arguments should match the parameters in the function definition. When we call functions in this way, the order (position) of the arguments can be changed.

Example:

both keyword arguments by changing their order student(age=13, name='Kelly')

Output: Student Details: Kelly 13

3. Positional Arguments

Positional arguments are those arguments where values get assigned to the arguments by their position when the function is called. For example, the 1st positional argument must be 1st when the function is called. The 2nd positional argument needs to be 2nd when the function is called, etc.

By default, Python functions are called using the positional arguments.

Example: Program to subtract 2 numbers using positional arguments.

def add(a, b): print(a - b) add(50, 10) # Output 40 add(10, 50) # Output -40

Note: If you try to pass more arguments, you will get an error.

def add(a, b): print(a - b) add(105, 561, 4)

Output TypeError: add() takes 2 positional arguments but 3 were given

Important points to remember about function argument

Point 1: Default arguments should follow non-default arguments

Point 2: keyword arguments should follow positional arguments only.

Point 3: The order of keyword arguments is not important, but All the keyword arguments passed must match one of the arguments accepted by the function.

Point 4: No argument should receive a value more than once

4. Variable-length arguments

In Python, sometimes, there is a situation where we need to pass multiple arguments to the function. Such types of arguments are called arbitrary arguments or variable-length arguments. We use variable-length arguments if we don't know the number of arguments needed for the function in advance.

Types of Arbitrary Arguments:

- arbitrary positional arguments (*args)

- arbitrary keyword arguments (**kwargs)

The *args and **kwargs allow you to pass multiple positional arguments or keyword arguments to a function.

- ### *Arbitrary positional arguments (*args)*

We can declare a variable-length argument with the * **(asterisk)** symbol. Place an asterisk (*) before a parameter in the function definition to define an arbitrary positional argument. we can pass multiple arguments to the function. Internally all these values are represented in the form of a tuple. Let's understand the use of variable-length arguments with an example.

This is a simple function that takes three arguments and returns their average:

def percentage(sub1, sub2, sub3): avg = (sub1 + sub2 + sub3) / 3 print('Average', avg)

percentage(56, 61, 73) This function works, but it's limited to only three arguments.

Example:

function with variable-length arguments

def percentage(*args): sum = 0 for i in args: # get total

sum = sum + i # calculate average avg = sum / len(args) print('Average =', avg) percentage(56, 61, 73)

Output: Average = 63.33

Note: args is just a name. You can choose any name that you prefer, such as *subjects.

- ### *Arbitrary keyword arguments (**kwargs)*

We saw how to use *args. Now let's see how to use the **kwargs argument. The **kwargs allow you to pass multiple keyword arguments to a function. Use the **kwargs if you want to handle named arguments in a function. Use the unpacking operator(**) to define variable-length keyword arguments. Keyword arguments passed to a kwargs are accessed using key-value pair (same as accessing a dictionary in Python).

Example:

function with variable-length keyword arguments

def percentage(**kwargs): sum = 0 for sub in kwargs:

get argument name sub_name = sub # get argument value

sub_marks = kwargs[sub] print(sub_name, "=", sub_marks)

pass multiple keyword arguments percentage(math=56, english=61, science=73)

Output: math = 56 english = 61 science = 73

3.2.3 Scope of Variables

In Python, we can declare variables in two different scopes: local scope and global scope.

A variable scope specifies the region where we can access a variable. For example,

def add_numbers(): sum = 5 + 4

Here, the sum variable is created inside the function, so it can only be accessed within it (local scope). This type of variable is called a local variable.

Based on the scope, we can classify Python variables into two types:

1. Local Variables
2. Global Variables

1.Python Local Variables

When we declare variables inside a function, these variables will have a local scope (within the function). We cannot access them outside the function. These types of variables are called local variables. For example,

def greet(): # local variable message = 'Hello' print('Local', message) greet()

try to access message variable # outside greet() function print(message)

Output

Local Hello NameError: name 'message' is not defined

2.Python Global Variables

In Python, a variable declared outside of the function or in global scope is known as a global variable. This means that a global variable can be accessed inside or outside of the function. Let's see an example of how a global variable is created in Python.

declare global variable message = 'Hello' def greet():

declare local variable print('Local', message) greet() print('Global', message)

Output

Local Hello Global Hello

declare global variable message = 'Hello' Now, message will be accessible from any scope (region) of the program.

3.2.4 Recursion

Recursion is the process of defining something in terms of itself. A physical world example would be to place two parallel mirrors facing each other. Any object in between them would be reflected recursively.

Python Recursive Function

In Python, we know that a function can call other functions. It is even possible for the function to call itself. These types of construct are termed as recursive functions. The following image shows the working of a recursive function called recurse.

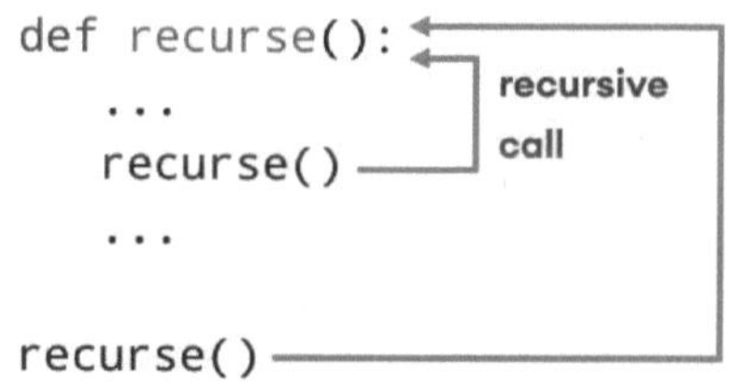

```
def recurse():
    ...
    recurse()
    ...

recurse()
```


Fig-Flow Chart for Recursion

Following is an example of a recursive function to find the factorial of an integer.

Factorial of a number is the product of all the integers from 1 to that number. For example, the factorial of 6 (denoted as 6!) is 1*2*3*4*5*6 = 720.

Example of a recursive function

def factorial(x): """This is a recursive function to find the factorial of an integer"""

if x == 1: return 1 else: return (x * factorial(x-1)) num = 3 print("The factorial of", num, "is", factorial(num))

Output The factorial of 3 is 6

factorial(3)

1st call with 3 3 * factorial(2) # 2nd call with 2 3 * 2 * factorial(1) # 3rd call with 1 3 * 2 * 1

return from 3rd call as number=1 3 * 2 # return from 2nd call 6 # return from 1st call

Let's look at an image that shows a step-by-step process of what is going on:

def recursor():

recursor(). recursor()

Output

Traceback (most recent call last): File "<string>",

line 3, in <module> File "<string>", line 2, in a File "<string>", line 2, in a File "<string>",

line 2, in a [Previous line repeated 996 more times] RecursionError: maximum recursion depth exceeded

Advantages of Recursion

1. Recursive functions make the code look clean and elegant.
2. A complex task can be broken down into simpler sub-problems using recursion.
3. Sequence generation is easier with recursion than using some nested iteration.

Disadvantages of Recursion

1. Sometimes the logic behind recursion is hard to follow through.
2. Recursive calls are expensive (inefficient) as they take up a lot of memory and time.
3. Recursive functions are hard to debug.

3.3 Strings

Strings are amongst the most popular types in Python. Creating strings is as simple as assigning a value to a variable. Python provides a rich set of operators, functions, and methods for working with strings, which helps access and extract portions of strings and manipulate and modify string data.Technically speaking, an **immutable data sequence** is known as a string in Python. In simple words, as discussed in the case of a crossword, a Python string is nothing but an array of characters, but a computer does not understand characters. It only understands the language of 0's and 1's.

3.3.1 Creating a String in Python

A string in Python can be easily created using single, double, or even triple quotes. The characters that form the string are enclosed within any of these quotes.

Code:

single_string='Hello' double_string="Hello World" triple_string="""Welcome to Scaler"""

print(single_string) print(double_string) print(triple_string)

Output: Hello Hello World Welcome to Scaler

3.3.2 Reassigning Strings in Python

Since strings in Python are immutable, we can update the values of strings simply by reassigning these strings with new values. The strings cannot be partially replaced, so it is always replaced completely with a new string. Let's see how that's done –

Code:

message="Welcome to Scaler" print(message)

message="Hello World" #reassigning a new string print(message)

Output: Welcome to Scaler Hello World

3.3.3 Accessing Strings in Python

The two primary ways of accessing characters of a string in Python are-

1. Indexing

The length of a string can be easily calculated using the len() function. The length of a string provides us with a range of the string. In python, we can perform indexing on any string as long as it is within the range. The index is always referred to as an integer. Using any other data type would give rise to a TypeError. Indexing can either be positive or negative. Positive indexing starts from 0 and indexing from the beginning of the string. On the other hand, negative indexing starts from -1, and indexing starts from the end of the string. Come and explore how indexing works by looking at the following example –

message="Welcome to Scaler" len_str= len(message) print(len_str) print(message[4])

positive indexing within the range print(message[-2])

#negative indexing within the range print(message[33])

#indexing outside the range

Output – 17 o e Traceback (most recent call last) : File "main.py", line 6, in <module> print (message [33]) #indexing outside the range IndexError: string index out of range

2. Slicing

Unlike indexing, slicing returns a range of characters using the slicing syntax.

The syntax looks like this – 'str[start_index: end_index]'

While performing slicing operations, one thing to remember is that the start index value is always included while that of the last index is always excluded.

Code:

message="Welcome to Scaler" print(message[2:5]) # positive slicing print(message[-10:-2])

#negative slicing print(message[:5]) #slicing from the start print(message[2:]) #slicing to the end

Output:

lco to scal welco lcome to Scaler

3.3.4 How to delete a string?

We have established that strings are immutable. In simple words, it means that once a string is assigned, we cannot make any changes to it. We cannot remove or delete any character of the string. What we can do is delete the Python string entirely. We can do so by using the del keyword.

The following code snippet shows how we can do that –

message="Welcome to Scaler" print(message) del message

print(message) The output is – Welcome to Scaler

Traceback (most recent call last) : File "main.py", line 4, in <module> print (message) NameError: name 'message' is not defined

3.3.5 Functions and Methods of Strings

STRING FUNCTIONS AND METHODS Python offers many built-in function for string manipulation. One method len() we have already used. Let us understand other methods also. To use string manipulation function the

Syntax is:

String_Object.functionName()

STRING FUNCTIONS/METHODS

- len(string) : this function returns the number of characters in any string including spaces.
- capitalize() : this function is used to convert the first letter of sentence in capital letter.
- title() : this function is used to convert first letter of every word in string in capital letters.
- upper() : this function is used to convert the entire string in capital letter.
- lower() : this function is used to convert the entire string in small letter.
- count(substring, [start,[end]]) : this function is used to find the number of occurrence of substring in our string.
- find(substring,[start,[end]]) : this function returns the index position of substring in the given string. We can also specify start and end index just like count() to modify search criteria. It return -1 if substring not found/
- index(substring) : this function return index position of substring. If substring not it returns error 'substring not found'
- isalnum() : this function is used to check where string contain all character as alphanumeric or not. Its return is either True or False.
- islower(): this function return True if all the characters in string is in small letters
- isupper() : this function return True if all the characters in string is in capital letters. Both islower() and isupper() will check the case only for letter, if any symbol present in string it will be ignored.
- isspace() :.it return True if the string contains only space.
- isalpha() : it return True if all the characters in string is alphabet.

- isdigit() : it returns True if all the characters in string is digit.
- split() : this function is used to split the string based on delimiter and store the result in the form of list. Default delimiter is space.
- partition(sep) : this function divides the string in the form of tuples of 3 elements known as head, sep and tail. All the string before sep becomes head and all the string after sep becomes tail. If sep is not present in the string then everything will becomes head, sep and tail will be empty.
- strip([chars]) : it return a copy of string with leading and trailing whitespaces removed. If chars is given, it remove characters instead.
- lstrip([chars]) : it return a copy of string with leading whitespaces removed. If chars is given, it remove characters instead.
- rstrip([chars]) : it return a copy of string with trailing whitespaces removed. If chars is given, it remove characters instead.

3.4 String Modules

This module is intended to provide access to basic string functions. Most of the functions provided here can be invoked with named parameters, unnamed parameters, or a mixture. Depending on the intended use, it may be advantageous to either preserve or remove such whitespace. This module will help you quickly access some string constants. Here's an example:

>>> import string >>> string.digits '0123456789' >>> string.ascii_lowercase

'abcdefghijklmnopqrstuvwxyz'

Here are some useful constants:

1.string.ascii_letters - The concatenation of the ascii_lowercase and ascii_uppercase constants described below. This value is not locale-dependent.

2.string.ascii_lowercase - The lowercase letters 'abcdefghijklmnopqrstuvwxyz'. This value is not locale-dependent and will not change.

3.string.ascii_uppercase - The uppercase letters 'ABCDEFGHIJKLMNOPQRSTUVWXYZ'. This value is not locale-dependent and will not change.

4.string.digits - The string '0123456789'.

5.string.hexdigits - The string '0123456789abcdefABCDEF'.

CHAPTER FOUR

LIST TUPLES AND DICTIONARIES

Introduction

Python has several other important data types that you'll probably use every day. They are called lists, tuples and dictionaries. This chapter's aim is to get you acquainted with each of these data types. They are not particularly complicated, so I expect that you will find learning how to use them very straight forward. Once you have mastered these three data types plus the string data type from the previous chapter, you will be quite a ways along in your education of Python. You'll be using these four building blocks in 99% of all the applications you will write. Well this data types were already introduced in before topics. And now we will learn about them in detail.

4.1 List

The List is like a dynamic array, along with the linear sequence, and also provides you with several built-in functions to perform various operations on data stored in it. Lists in Python can contain duplicate elements as each element is identified by a unique number/ position known as an index.

4.1.1 Operations of List

1. Indexing 2.Slicing 3.Concatenation 4.Repetitions 5.Updating 6. Membership 7.Comparison

1. Indexing

We can access the elements of a python list using the indexes — [0], [1], etc. The index starts at 0, so the index of the 'n'th element of a list is 'n-1'.

NUM_LIST =	[1,	2,	3,	4]
INDEX =	0	1	2	3

Fig-Explaining the indexing in list.

NUM_LIST =	[1,	2,	3,	4]
INDEX =	-4	-3	-2	-1

Fig-Explaining the negative indexing in list.

2.Slicing

A *slice* is a subset of list elements. In the case of lists, a single slice will always be of contiguous elements. Slice notation takes the form

my_list[*start*:*stop*]

where *start* is the index of the first element to include, and *stop* is the index of the item to stop at *without including it in the slice.* So my_list[1:5] returns ['b', 'c', 'd', 'e']: 0 *1 2 3 4* 5 6 7 8 × ↓ ↓ ↓ ↓ × × × × ['a', *'b', 'c', 'd', 'e'*, 'f', 'g', 'h', 'i']

3. Concatenation

In general, Concatenation is the process of joining the elements of a particular data-structure in an end-to-end manner.

The following are the 6 ways to concatenate lists in Python.

1.concatenation (+) operator 2.Naive Method 3.List Comprehension 4.extend() method 5. '*' operator 6.itertools.chain() method

i. Concatenation operator (+) for List Concatenation- The '+' operator can be used to concatenate two lists. It appends one list at the end of the other list and results in a new list as output.

ii. Naive Method for List Concatenation- In the Naive method, a for loop is used to traverse the second list. After this, the elements from the second list get appended to the first list. The **first list** results out to be the concatenation of the first and the second list.

iii. List Comprehension to concatenate lists - Python List Comprehension is an alternative method to concatenate two lists in Python. List Comprehension is basically the process of building/generating a list of elements based on an existing list. It uses for loop to process and traverses the list in an element-wise fashion. The below inline for-loop is equivalent to a nested for loop.

iv.Python extend() method for List Concatenation- Python's extend() method can be used to concatenate two lists in Python. The extend() function does iterate over the passed parameter and adds the item to the list thus, extending the list in a linear fashion.

Syntax: list.extend(iterable)

v. Python '*' operator for List Concatenation- Python's '*' operator can be used to easily concatenate two lists in Python. The '*' operator in Python basically **unpacks the collection of items** at the index arguments.

vi. Python itertools.chain() method to concatenate lists- Python itertools modules' itertools.chain() function can also be used to concatenate lists in Python. The itertools.chain() function accepts different iterables such as lists, string, tuples, etc as parameters and gives a sequence of them as output.

4. Repetition

We are accustomed to using the * symbol to represent multiplication, but when the operand on the left side of the * is a list, it becomes the repetition operator.

5. Membership

Python offers two membership operators to check or validate the membership of a value. It tests for membership in a sequence, such as strings, lists, or tuples.

in operator: The 'in' operator is used to check if a character/ substring/ element exists in a sequence or not. Evaluate to True if it finds the specified element in a sequence otherwise false

'not in' operator- Evaluates to true if it does not finds a variable in the specified sequence and false otherwise.

Identity operators

Identity operators are used to compare the objects if both the objects are actually of the same data type and share the same memory location. There are different identity operators such as

'is' operator – Evaluates to True if the variables on either side of the operator point to the same object and false **otherwise**

Output - True

6.Comparision

The list in python is a collection of similar items. We may at times need to compare data items in the two lists to perform certain operations. We will discuss certain methods to compare two lists in python. **Using list.sort() and == operator** -The list.sort() method sorts the two lists and the == operator compares the two lists item by item which means they have equal data items at equal positions. This checks if the list contains equal data item values but it does not take into account the order of elements in the list. This means that the list [1,2,3] will be equal to the list [2,1,3] according to this method of comparison.

7.Updation

You can update single or multiple elements of lists by giving the slice on the left-hand side of the assignment operator, and you can add to elements in a list with the append() method.

4.1.2 List Slices

List slicing is an operation that extracts a subset of elements from an list and packages them as another list.

Syntax:

Listname[start:stop]

Listname[start:stop:steps]

Points to remember while slicing a list:

1.default start value is 0 2.default stop value is n-1 3. [:] this will print the entire list 4. [2:2] this will create a empty slice

4.1.3List methods:

Methods used in lists are used to manipulate the data quickly. These methods work only on lists. They do not work on the other sequence types that are not mutable, that is, the values they contain cannot be changed, added, or deleted

syntax:

list name.method name(element/index/list)

The below methods have different functionalities which are described in their description.

	syntax	example	description

1	a.append(element)	>>> a=[1,2,3,4,5]
		>>> a.append(6)
		>>> print(a)
		[1, 2, 3, 4, 5, 6]
			Add an element to the end of the list

2	a.insert(index,element)	>>> a.insert(0,0)
		>>> print(a)
		[0, 1, 2, 3, 4, 5, 6]
			Insert an item at the defined index

3	a.extend(b)	>>> b=[7,8,9]
		>>> a.extend(b)
		>>> print(a)
		[0, 1, 2, 3, 4, 5, 6, 7, 8,9]
			Add all elements of a list to the another list

4	a.index(element)	>>> a.index(8) 8	Returns the index of the first matched item

5	a.sort()	>>> a.sort()
		>>> print(a)
		[0, 1, 2, 3, 4, 5, 6, 7, 8]
			Sort items in a list in ascending order

6	a.reverse()	>>> a.reverse()
		>>> print(a)
		[8, 7, 6, 5, 4, 3, 2, 1, 0]
			Reverse the order of items in the list

Fig- Representation of python list methods with their functionalities.

4.1.4 List loops:

1.For loop 2.While loop 3.Infinite loop

1. List using For Loop:

Loop continues until we reach the last item in the sequence.The body of for loop is separated from the rest of the code using indentation.

Syntax:

for val in sequence:

Statements

Accessing element	output
a=[10,20,30,40,50] for i in a: print(i)	1 2 3 4 5
Accessing index	**output**
a=[10,20,30,40,50] for i in range(0,len(a),1): print(i)	0 1 2 3 4
Accessing element using range:	**output**
a=[10,20,30,40,50] for i in range(0,len(a),1): print(a[i])	10 20 30 40 50

Fig-Accessing a list in different ways

2. List using While loop

When the condition is tested and the result is false, the loop body will be skipped and the first statement after the while loop will be executed.

Syntax:

while (condition):

body of while

Sum of elements in list

a=[1,2,3,4,5]

i=0,sum=0

while i<len(a): sum=sum+a[i]

i=i+1,print(sum)

Output:

15

3. Infinite Loop

A loop becomes infinite loop if the condition given never becomes false. It keeps on running. Such loops are called infinite loop.

4.1.5 Mutability:

Lists are mutable. (can be changed). Mutability is the ability for certain types of data to be changed without entirely recreating it.An item can be changed in a list by accessing it directly as part of the assignment statement. Using the indexing operator (square brackets[ ]) on the left side of an assignment, one of the list items can be updated.

4.1.6 Aliasing(copying):

Creating a copy of a list is called aliasing. When you create a copy both list will be having same memory location.

Example	Output:
a= [1, 2, 3 ,4 ,5]	
b=a	
print (b)	[1, 2, 3, 4, 5]
a is b	True
a[0]=100	
print(a)	[100,2,3,4,5]
print(b)	[100,2,3,4,5]

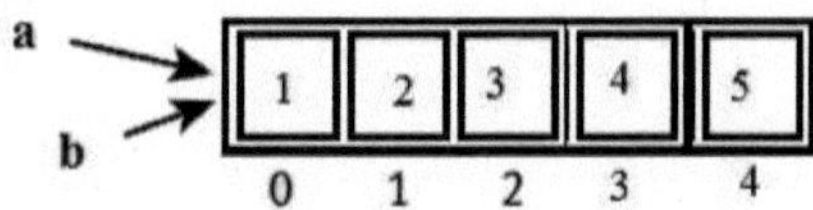

Fig- Example of Alaising in list.

This type of change is what is known as a **side effect**. This happens because after the assignment **b=a,** the variables **a** and **b** refer to the exact same list object. They are **aliases** for the same object. This phenomenon is known as **aliasing**. To prevent aliasing, a new object can be created and the contents of the original can be copied which is called **cloning.**

4.1.7 Clonning:

To avoid the disadvantages of copying we are using cloning. creating a copy of a same list of elements with two different memory locations is called cloning. Changes in one list will not affect locations of another list. Cloning is a process of making a copy of the list without modifying the original list.

1.Slicing 2.list()method 3.copy() method

4.1.8 List as parameters:

In python, arguments are passed by reference. If any changes are done in the parameter which refers within the function, then the changes also reflects back in the calling function. When a list to a function is passed, the function gets a reference to the list. Since lists are mutable, changes made to the elements referenced by the parameter change the same list that the argument is referencing.

4.2 Tuples

A tuple is same as list, except that the set of elements is enclosed in parentheses instead of square brackets.A tuple is an immutable list. i.e. once a tuple has been created, you can't add elements to a tuple or remove elements from the tuple.But tuple can be converted into list and list can be converted in to tuple.

methods	example	description

list( )	>>> a=(1,2,3,4,5)
	>>> a=list(a)
	>>> print(a)
	[1, 2, 3, 4, 5]
		it convert the given tuple into list.

tuple( )	>>> a=[1,2,3,4,5]
	>>> a=tuple(a)
	>>> print(a)
	(1, 2, 3, 4, 5)
		it convert the given list into tuple.

Fig-Conversion of tuple to list

Benefit of Tuple:

Tuples are faster than lists.If the user wants to protect the data from accidental changes, tuple can be used.Tuples can be used as keys in dictionaries, while lists can't.

4.2.1 Operations on Tuples:

1.Indexing 2.Slicing 3.Concatenation 4.Repetitions 5.Membership 6.Comparison

1.Indexing

The indexing and slicing in tuple are similar to lists. The indexing in the tuple starts from 0 and goes to length (tuple) – 1. The items in the tuple can be accessed by using the slice operator. Python also allows us to use the colon operator to access multiple items in the tuple.

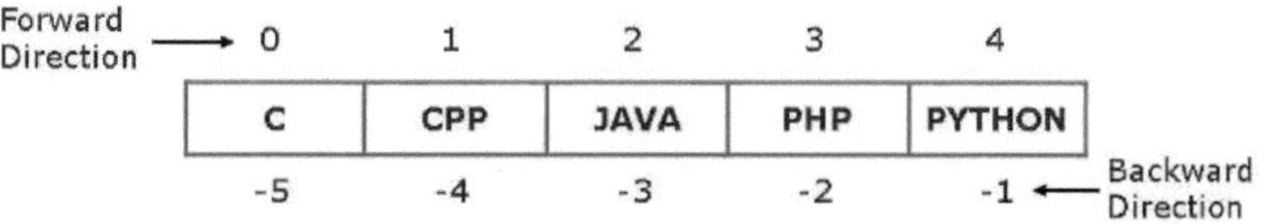

Fig- Indexing in Tuple

2.Slicing- Tuple slicing is a frequent practice in Python, and it is the most prevalent technique used by programmers to solve efficient problems. Consider a Python tuple. You must slice a tuple in order to access a range of elements in it. One method is to utilize the colon as a simple slicing operator (:).The slice operator allows you to specify where to begin slicing, where to stop slicing, and what step to take. Tuple slicing creates a new tuple from an old one.

Syntax

tuple[Start : Stop : Stride]. The expression returns the portion of the tuple from index Start to index Stop, at a step size Stride.

3.Concatenation- Many times, while working with records, we can have a problem in which we need to add two records and store them together. This requires concatenation. As tuples are immutable, this task becomes little complex. Let's discuss certain ways in which this task can be performed.

Method #1 : Using + operator This is the most Pythonic and recommended method to perform this particular task. In this, we add two tuples and return the concatenated tuple. No previous tuple is changed in this process.

Method #2 : Using sum() This is yet another way in which this task can be performed. In this, we add the tuples to one other using sum function.

Operations	examples	description
Creating a tuple	>>>a=(20,40,60,"apple","ball")	Creating the tuple with elements of different data types.
Indexing	>>>print(a[0]) 20 >>> a[2] 60	Accessing the item in the position 0 Accessing the item in the position 2
Slicing	>>>print(a[1:3]) (40,60)	Displaying items from 1st till 2nd.
Concatenation	>>> b=(2,4) >>>print(a+b) >>>(20,40,60,"apple","ball",2,4)	Adding tuple elements at the end of another tuple elements
Repetition	>>>print(b*2) >>>(2,4,2,4)	repeating the tuple in n no of times

Membership	>>> a=(2,3,4,5,6,7,8,9,10)
	>>> 5 in a
	True
	>>> 100 in a
	False
	>>> 2 not in a
	False
		Returns True if element is present in tuple. Otherwise returns false.

Comparison	>>> a=(2,3,4,5,6,7,8,9,10)
	>>>b=(2,3,4)
	>>> a==b
	False
	>>> a!=b
	True
		Returns True if all elements in both elements are same. Otherwise returns false

Fig-Operations on Tuple

4.2.2 Tuple methods:

Tuple is immutable so changes cannot be done on the elements of a tuple once it is assigned.

methods	example	description

a.index(tuple)	>>> a=(1,2,3,4,5)
	>>> a.index(5)
	4
		Returns the index of the first matched item.

a.count(tuple)	>>>a=(1,2,3,4,5) >>> a.count(3) 1	Returns the count of the given element.
len(tuple)	>>> len(a) 5	return the length of the tuple
min(tuple)	>>> min(a) 1	return the minimum element in a tuple
max(tuple)	>>> max(a) 5	return the maximum element in a tuple
del(tuple)	>>> del(a)	Delete the entire tuple.

Fig- Some Methods on Tuple

4.2.3 Tuple Assignment:

Tuple assignment allows, variables on the left of an assignment operator and values of tuple on the right of the assignment operator.Multiple assignment works by creating a tuple of expressions from the right hand side, and a tuple of targets from the left, and then matching each expression to a target.

Example:

Swapping using tuple assignment:

```
a=20

b=50

(a,b)=(b,a)

print("value after swapping is",a,b)
```

4.2.4 Tuple as return value:

A Tuple is a comma separated sequence of items.It is created with or without ( ).A function can return one value. if you want to return more than one value from a function. we can use tuple as return value.

Example1:

```
def div(a,b): r=a%b,q=a//b

return(r,q)

a=eval(input("enter a value:"))

b=eval(input("enter b value:"))

r,q=div(a,b)

print("reminder:",r)

print("quotient:",q)
```

Output:

enter a value:4 enter b value:3 reminder: 1 quotient: 1

4.2.5 Tuple as argument:

The parameter name that begins with * gathers argument into a tuple.

Example:

def printall(*args): print(args) printall(2,3,'a')

Output:

(2, 3, 'a')

4.3 Dictionaries

Dictionary is an unordered collection of elements. An element in dictionary has a key: value pair.All elements in dictionary are placed inside the curly braces i.e. { }Elements in Dictionaries are **accessed via keys** and not by their position.The values of a dictionary can be any data type.Keys must be immutable data type (numbers, strings, tuple).

4.3.1. Operations

1.Accessing an element 2.Update 3.Add element 4.Membership

1.Accessing Values in Dictionary

To access dictionary elements, you can use the familiar square brackets along with the key to obtain its value. Following is a simple example –

dict = {'Name': 'Zara', 'Age': 7, 'Class': 'First'}

print("dict['Name']: ", dict['Name']) print ("dict['Age']: ", dict['Age'])

When the above code is executed, it produces the following result – dict['Name']: Zara dict['Age']: 7

2.Updating Dictionary

You can update a dictionary by adding a new entry or a key-value pair, modifying an existing entry, or deleting an existing entry as shown below in the simple example –

dict = {'Name': 'Zara', 'Age': 7, 'Class': 'First'} dict['Age'] = 8;

update existing entry

dict['School'] = "DPS School" # Add new entry

print ("dict['Age']: ", dict['Age']) print ("dict['School']: ", dict['School'])

When the above code is executed, it produces the following result – dict['Age']: 8 dict['School']: DPS School

3. Update Dictionary

The syntax for adding items to a dictionary is the same as the syntax we used when updating an item. The only difference here is that the index key will include the name of the new key to be created and its corresponding value.

Here's what the syntax looks like: devBio[**newKey**] = **newValue.**

We can also use the update() method to add new items to a dictionary. Here's what that would look like: devBio.**update**({"**newKey**": **newValue**}).

4. Membership

Dictionaries are common and extensively used data types in python. They are used to store key-value pairs and these values are accessed by their respective keys.

Using the in operator to check if key exists in dictionary python:

In this method, we use the membership operator; in. This operator is used to check if one value is a member of another. It returns a boolean value.

Code to check if a key exists in dictionary in python:

dict_1 = {"a": 1, "b":2, "c":3} if "a" in dict_1:

print("Exists") else:

print("Does not exist") #Output = "Exists"

Similarly, the not in operator can also be used to check if a key does not exist in a dictionary.

4.3.2 Methods in dictionary:

The following is an overview of methods that apply to dictionaries:

1. d.clear()-Clears a dictionary. d.clear() empties dictionary d of all key-value pairs:

2. d.get(<key>[, <default>])- Returns the value for a key if it exists in the dictionary. The Python dictionary .get() method provides a convenient way of getting the value of a key from a dictionary without checking ahead of time whether the key exists, and without raising an error.

3. d.items() - Returns a list of key-value pairs in a dictionary. d.items() returns a list of tuples containing the key-value pairs in d. The first item in each tuple is the key, and the second item is the key's value:

4. d.keys()- Returns a list of keys in a dictionary. d.keys() returns a list of all keys in d:

5. d.values() - Returns a list of values in a dictionary. d.values() returns a list of all values in d:

6.d.pop(<key>[, <default>]) - Removes a key from a dictionary, if it is present, and returns its value. If <key> is present in d, d.pop(<key>) removes <key> and returns its associated value:

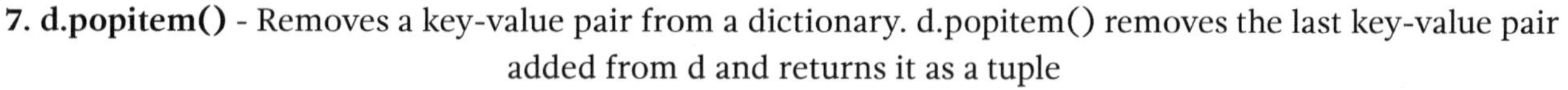

7. d.popitem() - Removes a key-value pair from a dictionary. d.popitem() removes the last key-value pair added from d and returns it as a tuple

8. **d.update(<obj>)**-Merges a dictionary with another dictionary or with an iterable of key-value pairs.Here is an example showing two dictionaries merged together

4.4 Advanced list processing:

4.4.1 List Comprehension:

List comprehensions provide a concise way to apply operations on a list.It creates a new list in which each element is the result of applying a given operation in a list.It consists of brackets containing an expression followed by a "for" clause, then a list.The list comprehension always returns a result list.

Syntax

list=[expression for item in list if conditional]

How to use list comprehension in Python

Using the same example from earlier on, here is how you'd create a new list of numbers from 0 - 4 with the range() function in just one single line, using list comprehension:

new_list = [num for num in range(5)] print(new_list) #output #[0, 1, 2, 3, 4]

This has the same output as the for loop example, but with significantly less code!

How to use conditionals with list comprehension in Python

Optionally, you can use an if statement with a list comprehension. The general syntax looks like this:

new_list = [expression for variable in iterable if condition == True]

Conditionals act as a filter and add an extra check for additional precision and customisation when creating a new list. This means that the value in the expression has to meet certain criteria and a certain condition you speficy, in order to go in the new list.

new_list = [num for num in range(50) if num % 2 == 0]

print(new_list)

#output #[0, 2, 4, 6, 8, 10, 12, 14, 16, 18, 20, 22, 24, 26, 28, 30, 32, 34, 36, 38, 40, 42, 44, 46, 48]

In the example above, only the values where the condition num % 2 == 0 is checked and evaluates to True will enter new_list.The values that don't meet the conditions are excluded and are not added.

How to use list comprehension on strings in Python

You can create a new list with the individual characters contained in a given string.

```
fave_language_chars = [letter for letter in "Python"]

print(fave_language_chars)

#output #['P', 'y', 't', 'h', 'o', 'n']
```

The new list that gets created is comprised of all the separate letters contained in the string "Python", which acts as an iterable.

4.5 Illustrative Problems

1.simple sorting

arr=[5,2,8,7,1] temp=0

#Displaying elements of original array

print("Elements of original array: ")

for i in range(0, len(arr)):

print(arr[i], end="")

#Sort the array in ascending order

for i in range(0, len(arr)): for j in range(i+1, len(arr)):

if(arr[i] > arr[j]): temp=arr[i] arr[i]=arr[j] arr[j]=temp print()

#Displaying elements of the array after sorting

print("Elements of array sorted in ascending order:")

for i in range(0,len(arr)): print(arr[i],end="")

Output:

Elements of original array: 5 2 8 7 1

Elements of array sorted in ascending order: 1 2 5 7 8

2.Histogram

def histogram(items):

for n in items: output = '' times = n

while(times > 0): output += '*' times = times - 1 print(output) histogram([2, 3, 6, 5])

Output :

**

***

******

*****

3.Students marks statement

class Student(object):

def __init__(self, name, roll, marks): self.name = name self.roll = roll

self.marks = marks def getmarks(self): return self.marks

def getroll(self): return self.roll def __str__(self):

return self.name + ' : ' + str(self.getroll()) +' ::'+ str(self.getmarks())

def Markss(rec, name, roll, marks): rec.append(Student(name, roll, marks))

return rec # Main Code Record = [] x = 'y'

while x == 'y':

name = input('Enter the name of the student: ')

height = input('Enter the roll number: ')

roll = input('Marks: ')

Record = Markss(Record, name, roll, height)

x = input('another student? y/n: ')

Printing the list of student

n = 1

for el in Record:

print(n,'. ', el)

n = n + 1

Output

Enter the name of the student: Bharath Enter the roll number: 201 Marks: 300

another student? y/n: y Enter the name of the student: Shivangi Enter the roll number: 202

Marks: 320 another student? y/n: y Enter the name of the student: Vrusha Enter the roll number: 203

Marks: 350 another student? y/n: n 1 . Bharath : 300 ::201 2 . Shivangi : 320 ::202 3 . Vrusha : 350 ::203

4.Retail bill preparation.

customer = str(input("Customer's name: "))

print ("Welcome to our store") print ("This is our products") print ("orange 0.5$) print ("Apple 1$)

print ("Grape 0.5$) print ("Banana 0.5$) chooseproducts= int(input("What do you want to buy: "))

Output:

BILL Orange 5 2.5$ Apple 3 3$ Grape 2 1$ Total: 10 6.5$

CHAPTER FIVE

FILES, MODULES, PACKAGES

Introduction

If you quit from the Python interpreter and enter it again, the definitions you have made (functions and variables) are lost. Therefore, if you want to write a somewhat longer program, you are better off using a text editor to prepare the input for the interpreter and running it with that file as input instead. This is known as creating a *script*. To support this, Python has a way to put definitions in a file and use them in a script or in an interactive instance of the interpreter. Such a file is called a *module*; definitions from a module can be *imported* into other modules or into the *main* module (the collection of variables that you have access to in a script executed at the top level and in calculator mode).A **library** is an umbrella term that loosely means “a bundle of code.”The Python Standard Library contains hundreds of modules for performing common tasks, like sending emails or reading JSON data.

5.1 Files

Python too supports file handling and allows users to handle files i.e., to read and write files, along with many other file handling options, to operate on files. Python treats files differently as text or binary and this is important. Each line of code includes a sequence of characters and they form a text file.

1.
Text files:

In this type of file, Each line of text is terminated with a special character called EOL (End of Line), which is the new line character ('\n') in python by default. Text file store the data in the form of characters. Text file are used to store characters or strings. Usually we can use text files to store character data eg: abc.txt

2. Binary File :

Binary files: In this type of file, there is no terminator for a line, and the data is stored after converting it into machine-understandable binary language. Binary file store entire data in the form of bytes. Binary file can be used to store text, image, audio and video.

Opening a File

Before performing any operation (like read or write) on the file,first we have to open that file.For this we should use Python's inbuilt function open(). This function accepts 'filename' and 'open mode' in which to open the file. file handler = open("file name", "open mode", "buffering")

- f = open(filename, mode)

The File Opening Mode

w- To write data into file. If any data is already present in the file, it would be deleted and the present data will be stored. open an existing file for write operation.

r- To read the data form the file. The file pointer is positioned at the beginning of the file.open an existing file for read operation. The file pointer is positioned at the beginning of the file.

a-To append data to the file. Appending means adding at the end of existing data. The file pointer is placed at the end of the file.

w+ -To write and read data a file. The previous data in the file will be deleted. To write and read data. It will override existing data.

r+ -To read and write data into the file. The previous data in the file will not be deleted.The file pointer is placed at the beginning of the file.

a+ - To append and read data from the file.It wont override existing data.

x-To open a file in exclusive creation mode for write operation. If the file already exists then we will get FileExistsError.

- **f = open("abc.txt","w")**

We are opening abc.txt file for writing data.

5.1.1 Reading and Writing Files

Let's try out all the reading methods for reading from a file, and you will also explore the access modes along with it! There are three ways to read from a file.

- read([n])
- readline([n])
- readlines()

Here n is the number of bytes to be read. If nothing is passed to n, then the complete file is considered to be read. Create a file as below: 1st line 2nd line 3rd line 4th line 5th line Let's understand what each read method does:

my_file=open("test1.txt","r")

print(my_file.read())

1st line 2nd line 3rd line 4th line 5th line

The read() method just outputs the entire file if the number of bytes (n) is not given in the argument. If you execute my_file.read(3), you will get back the first three characters of the file, as shown below:

my_file=open("test1.txt","r")

print(my_file.read(3))

1st

readline(n)

outputs at most n bytes of a single line of a file. It does not read more than one line.

my_file.close()

my_file=open("test1.txt","r")

#Use print to print the line else will remain in buffer and replaced by next statement
print(my_file.readline())

outputs first two characters of next line

print(my_file.readline(2))

1st line 2n

Closing Python Files with close()

Use the close() method with file handle to close the file. When you use this method, you clear all buffer and close the file.

my_file.close()

5.1.2 Writing to a file

You can use three methods to write to a file in Python:

- write(string) (for text) or write(byte_string) (for binary)
- writelines(list)

Let's create a new file. The following will create a new file in the specified folder because it does not exist. Remember to give correct path with correct filename; otherwise, you will get an error: Create a notepad file and write some text in it. Make sure to save the file as .txt and save it to the working directory of Python.

new_file=open("newfile.txt",mode="w",encoding="utf-8")

new_file.write("Writing to a new file\n")

new_file.close()

1.Append Mode

Now let's write a list to this file with a+ mode:

fruits=["Orange\n","Banana\n","Apple\n"]

new_file=open("newfile.txt",mode="a+",encoding="utf-8")

new_file.writelines(fruits)

for line in new_file:

print(line)

new_file.close()

2.Seek Method

Note that reading from a file does not print anything because the file cursor is at the end of the file. To set the cursor at the beginning, you can use the seek() method of file object:

cars=["Audi\n","Bentley\n","Toyota\n"]

new_file=open("newfile.txt",mode="a+",encoding="utf-8")

for car in cars:

new_file.write(car)

print("Tell the byte at which the file cursor is:",new_file.tell())

new_file.seek(0)

for line in new_file:

print(line)

Tell the byte at which the file cursor is: 115 Writing to a new file Writing to a new file Writing to a new file Orange Banana Apple Audi Bentley Toyota.

Let's try out passing another reference point and offset and see the output:

new_file.seek(4,0) print(new_file.readline()) new_file.close() ing to a new file

3. next Method

You are only left with the next() method. Here you are using the same file created above with the name test1.txt. End-relative seeks such as seek(-2,2) are not allowed if file mode does not include 'b', which indicates binary format.

file=open("test1.txt","r") for index in range(5): line=next(file) print(line) file.close()

1st line 2nd line 3rd line 4th line 5th line

Note: write() method doesn't write data to a file, but to a buffer, it does, but only when the close() method is called.

5.1.3 Format Operator

Input from the keyboard and output to the screen are possible using the READ and PRINT statements. So far only list-directed input and output has been encountered, READ * and PRINT *. The information is placed in a FORMAT statement.

The Format Statement

The general form of the FORMAT statement is:

label - FORMAT(c,edl,ed2,'Text message to the screen',ed3...)

where

label->is a identifying number for PRINT or READ.

edl,ed2->are edit descriptors separated by commas

text-> messages are surrounded by single quotes

c ->is carriage control for OUTPUT only and can be:

lx ->moving the output to the next line

O ->double spacing the output

+ ->move to beginning of line, overwriting anything already there

1 ->start a new page

5.2 File Handling

5.2 .1 Formatted Input

Getting a formatted READ to work correctly is very tricky to do. Every blank specified in the FORMAT statement must be present and the values have to appear exactly as specified in the FORMAT statement. The only real advantage of doing a formatted READ iS that character variables do not need single quotes around them to be read in properly. There are no rules governing the location of FORMAT statements in programs except that they must be in the same local or sub program unit that refers to them. Format statements can be placed directly after PRINT and READ statements but some programmers prefer to keep them together near the end of a program.

5.2.2 Handling Files

So far the programs written have taken input data from the keyboard and the results have been displayed on the computer screen. The statements for input and output must include details of how and where to input data from and output to. READ * may be expanded to include these controls, however WRITE iS used for output rather than PRINT. Example Program 5 exemplifies common ways of dealing with files: opening, closing, reading from and writing to.

UNIT = unit identifier FMT = format identifier END = label ERR = label

Example:

READ(UNIT = l,FMT = 10)A,B,C READ(1,10)A,B,C WRITE(UNIT = 2,FMT = 20)X,Y,Z

WRITE(2,20)X,Y,Z

Unit identifier

Every control list must contain a unit identifier. It is this that identifies the location of the file or device to be accessed. If the unit identifier is first in the control list the UNIT = may be omitted. For example:

WRITE(2,FMT=20)X,Y,Z

You may choose any number for a unit identifier except for two reserved values that generally have predefined meanings.

Format identifier

This identifies how the data is organised either by reference to a FORMAT statement or an asterisk indicating list-directed format.

Example

READ(UNIT=l, FMT = 10)A,B,C The FORMAT statementitisatlabel l0

*READ(UNIT=1, FMT = *)A,B,C Asterisk (*) means list-directed forrnatting. In other words, no formatting*

If the format identifier is second in the control list the FMT = may be omitted.

5.2.3 End-of-file condition

Only one end-of-file condition may appear in the control list. When the READ statement reaches the end of the data file without an error occurring, no more data is transferred and the control of the program jumps to the label specified in the READ statement.

Error condition

If some error occurs on input/output and there is an error specifier, the input/output is stopped and the program jumps to the label given in the error specifier.

5.3 Command Line Arguments

A command line interface (CLI) is a program that is designed to allow users to interact with software on their computer. A command-line argument is an argument that gets passed into a program through the CLI by the user. Python **Command Line Arguments** provides a convenient way to accept some information at the command line while running the program. For example -

$ python script.py arg1 arg2 arg3

Here Python script name is **script.py** and rest of the three arguments - arg1 arg2 arg3 are command line arguments for the program. There are following three Python modules which are helpful in parsing and managing the command line arguments:

1. sys module 2. getopt.getopt method3.argparse module

1.sys module - System-specific parameters

The Python **sys** module provides access to any command-line arguments via the **sys.argv**. This serves two purposes –

- sys.argv is the list of command-line arguments.
- len(sys.argv) is the number of command-line arguments.

Here sys.argv[0] is the program ie. script name.

Example

Consider the following script test.py –

import sys

print ('Number of arguments:', len(sys.argv), 'arguments.')

print ('Argument List:', str(sys.argv))

Now run above script as below. All the programs in this tutorial need to be run from the command line, so we are unable to provide online compile & run option for these programs. Kindly try to run these programs at your computer.

$ python test.py arg1 arg2 arg3

This produce following result – Number of arguments: 4 arguments. Argument List: ['test.py', 'arg1', 'arg2', 'arg3']

Parsing Command-Line Arguments

Python provided a **getopt** module that helps you parse command-line options and arguments. This module provides two functions and an exception to enable command line argument parsing.

2. getopt.getopt method

This method parses command line options and parameter list. Following is simple syntax for this method –

getopt.getopt(args, options, [long_options])

args – This is the argument list to be parsed. **options** – This is the string of option letters that the script wants to recognize, with options that require an argument should be followed by a colon (:). **long_options** – This is optional parameter and if specified, must be a list of strings with the names of the long options, which should be supported. Long options, which require an argument should be followed by an equal sign ('='). To accept only long options, options should be an empty string.

3. Python argparse Module

Python **argparse** module makes it easy to write user-friendly command-line interfaces. The program defines what arguments it requires, and argparse will figure out how to parse those out of sys.argv. The argparse module also automatically generates help and usage messages.

5.4 Errors and Exceptions

An exception is an **event that occurs during the execution of programs that disrupt the normal flow of execution** (e.g., KeyError Raised when a key is not found in a dictionary.) An exception is a Python object that represents an error. In Python, an exception is an object derives from the **BaseException** class that contains information about an error event that occurred within a method. **Exception object contains:**

1.Error type (exception name) 2.The state of the program when the error occurred 3. An error message describes the error event.

Why use Exception

Standardized error handling: Using built-in exceptions or creating a custom exception with a more precise name and description, you can adequately define the error event, which helps you debug the error event. **Cleaner code**: Exceptions separate the error-handling code from regular code, which helps us to maintain large code easily. **Robust application**: With the help of exceptions, we can develop a solid application, which can handle error event efficiently **Exceptions propagation**: By default, the exception propagates the call stack if you don't catch it.

5.4.1 What are Errors?

On the other hand, An **error** is an action that is incorrect or inaccurate. For example, syntax error. Due to which the program fails to execute.

The errors can be broadly classified into two types:

1. Syntax errors Logical errors

1.Syntax error

The syntax error occurs when we are not following the proper structure or syntax of the language. A syntax error is also known as a **parsing error**. When Python parses the program and finds an incorrect statement it is known as a syntax error.

Common Python Syntax errors:-Incorrect indentation ,Missing colon, comma, or brackets, Putting keywords in the wrong place.

Example

```
print("Welcome to PYnative")

print "Learn Python with us.."
```

Output

print "Learn Python with us.."

^ IndentationError: unexpected indent

2. Logical errors (Exception)

Even if a statement or expression is syntactically correct, the error that occurs at the runtime is known as a **Logical error or Exception**. In other words, **Errors detected during execution are called exceptions.**

Common Python Logical errors:-Indenting a block to the wrong level,using the wrong variable name,making a mistake in a boolean expression

Example

a = 10 b = 20

print("Addition:", a + c)

Output

print("Addition:", a + c)

NameError: name 'c' is not defined

5.4.2 Built-in Exceptions

The below table shows different built-in exceptions.

Python automatically generates many exceptions and errors. Runtime exceptions, generally a result of programming errors, such as:

Reading a file that is not present.Trying to read data outside the available index of a list .Dividing an integer value by zero

Error vs. Exceptions

Error vs. Exceptions	
Error	**Exceptions**
All errors in Python are the unchecked type.	Exceptions include both checked and unchecked type.
Errors occur at run time which unknown to the compiler.	Exceptions can be recover by handling them with the help of try-catch blocks.
Errors are mostly caused by the environment in which an application is running.	The application itself causes exceptions.
Examples: OutofMemoryError	Examples: Checked Exceptions, SQL exception, NullPointerException,etc.

Table-2 : Difference between errors and exceptions

5.5 Handling Errors

In python or any other Programming Language it is important to handle errors .If these errors are not handled then they can cause huge loses.

5.5.1 Rules of Exceptions

Befor getting to handle exceptions we need to know some rules to handle them. Here are some essential rules of Python exception handling:

Exceptions must be class objects. For class exceptions, you can use try statement with an except clause which mentions a particular class. Even if a statement or expression is syntactically correct, it may display an error when an attempt is made to execute it. Errors found during execution are called exceptions, and they are not unconditionally fatal.

5.5.2 Python Exception Handling Mechanism

Exception handling is managed by the following 5 keywords:

1. try 2.except 3.finally 4.raise

1.Python Try Statement

A try statement includes keyword try, followed by a colon (:) and a suite of code in which exceptions may occur. It has one or more clauses. During the execution of the try statement, if no exceptions occurred then, the interpreter ignores the exception handlers for that specific try statement. In case, if any exception occurs in a try suite, the try suite expires and program control transfers to the matching except handler following the try suite.

Syntax:

try:

statement(s)

2.The except Statement

A try statement can have more than one except clause, to specify handlers for different exceptions. Please note that at most one handler will be executed. Handlers only handle exceptions that occur in the corresponding *try clause*, not in other handlers of the same try statement. The general **syntax** for adding specific exceptions are –

```
try:
# statement(s)
except IndexError:
# statement(s)
except ValueError:
# statement(s)
```

3.Finally Statement in Python

Finally block always executes irrespective of an exception being thrown or not. The final keyword allows you to create a block of code that follows a try-except block. Finally, clause is optional. It is intended to define clean-up actions which should be that executed in all conditions.

Syntax with Example

```
try:
raise KeyboardInterrupt
finally:
print 'welcome, world!'
```

Output

KeyboardInterrupt

Finally, clause is executed before try statement.

4. Raise Statement in Python

The raise statement specifies an argument which initializes the exception object. Here, a comma follows the exception name, and argument or tuple of the argument that follows the comma.

Syntax:

raise [Exception [, args [, traceback]]]

In this syntax, the argument is optional, and at the time of execution, the exception argument value is always none.

Example:

Look at the following example, which asks the user for input until a valid integer has been entered, but allows the user to interrupt the program.

```
while True:

try:

x = int(input("Please enter a number: "))

break

except ValueError:

print("Oops! That was no valid number. Try again...")
```

A class in an except clause is compatible with an exception if it is the same class or a base class thereof (but not the other way around — an *except clause* listing a derived class is not compatible with a base class). For example, the following code will print B, C, D in that order:

```
class B(Exception):pass

class C(B): pass class D(C): pass for cls in [B, C, D]:

try: raise cls() except D: print("D") except C: print("C") except B: print("B")
```

Output:B C D

5.5.3. Raising Exceptions

The raise statement allows the programmer to force a specified exception to occur. For example:

Example:

```
try: raise NameError('HiThere') except NameError:

print('An exception flew by!')

raise
```

Output:

An exception flew by! Traceback (most recent call last): File "<stdin>", line 2, in <module> NameError: HiThere

5.5.4. User-defined Exceptions

Programs may name their own exceptions by creating a new exception class. Exceptions should typically be derived from the Exception class, either directly or indirectly. Exception classes can be defined which do anything any other class can do, but are usually kept simple, often only offering a number of attributes that allow information about the error to be extracted by handlers for the exception.

5.5.5. Defining Clean-up Actions

The try statement has another optional clause which is intended to define clean-up actions that must be executed under all circumstances. For example:

try:

raise KeyboardInterrupt finally: print('Goodbye, world!')

Output:

Goodbye, world! ,KeyboardInterrupt Traceback (most recent call last): File "<stdin>", line 2, in <module>

If a finally clause is present, the finally clause will execute as the last task before the try statement completes. The finally clause runs whether or not the try statement produces an exception.

5.6 Modules

If you quit from the Python interpreter and enter it again, the definitions you have made (functions and variables) are lost. Therefore, if you want to write a somewhat longer program, you are better off using a text editor to prepare the input for the interpreter and running it with that file as input instead. This is known as creating a *script*. Such a file is called a *module*; definitions from a module can be *imported* into other modules or into the *main* module . Let's construct a module. Save the file as example_module.py after entering the following.

Code

#Python program to show how to create a module #Defining a function in the module to reuse

def square(number):

"""This function will square the number passed to it"""

result= number**2 return result

Here, a module called example_module contains the definition of the function square(). The function returns the square of a given number.

5.6.1 How to Import Modules in Python?

In Python, we may import functions from one module into our program, or as we say into, another module. For this, we make use of the import Python keyword called import.

Code

import example_module

The functions that we defined in the example_module are not immediately imported into the present program. Only the name of the module, i.e., example_ module, is imported here.

5.6.2 Python import Statement

Using the import Python keyword and the dot operator, we may import a standard module and can access the defined functions within it. Here's an illustration.

Code

#Python program to show how to import a standard module # We will import the math module which is a standard module import math print("The value of euler's number is",math.e)

Output:

The value of euler's number is 2.718281828459045

5.6.3 Python from...import Statement

We can import specific names from a module without importing the module as a whole. Here is an example.

Code

from math import e print("The value of euler's number is",e)

Output:

The value of euler's number is 2.718281828459045

5.6.4 Locating Path of Modules

The interpreter searches numerous places when importing a module in the Python program. Several directories are searched if the built-in module is not present. The list of directories can be accessed using sys.path.

5.6.5 The dir() Built-in Function

We may use the dir() method to identify names declared within a module.

For instance, we have the following names in the standard module str. To print the names, we will use the dir() method in the following way:

Code

#Python program to print the directory of a module ,print("List of functions:\n",dir(str), end=",")

Output:

List of functions: ['__add__', '__class__', '__contains__', '__delattr__', '__dir__', '__doc__', '__eq__', '__format__', '__ge__', '__getattribute__', '__getitem__', '__getnewargs__', '__gt__', '__hash__', '__init__', '__init_subclass__', '__iter__', '__le__', '__len__', '__lt__', '__mod__', '__mul__', '__ne__', '__new__', '__reduce__','rpartition', 'rsplit', 'rstrip', 'split', 'splitlines', 'startswith', 'strip', 'swapcase', 'title', 'translate', 'upper', 'zfill']

5.6.6 Namespaces and Scoping

Both local and global namespace variables can be accessed by a Python statement. When two variables with the same name are local and global, the local variable takes the role of the global variable.Python is informed that Var_Name is a global variable by the line global Var_Name. Python stops looking for the variable inside the local namespace. We declare the variable Number, for instance, within the global namespace. UnboundLocalError will be the outcome if we try to access the value of the local variable without or before declaring it global.

Code

Number=204 def AddNumber():

global Number Number = Number + 200 print(Number) AddNumber() print(Number)

Output: 204 404

5.7 Packages

We organize a large number of files in different folders and subfolders based on some criteria, so that we can find and manage them easily. As you know, a module can contain multiple objects, such as classes, functions, etc. A package can contain one or more relevant modules.

Let's create a package named mypackage, using the following steps:

Create a new folder named D:\MyApp. Inside MyApp, create a subfolder with the name 'mypackage'. Create an empty __init__.py file in the mypackage folder. Using a Python-aware editor like IDLE, create modules greet.py and functions.py with the following code:

1.Let the below function be saved as greet.py

```
def SayHello(name):
print("Hello ", name)
```

2. Now create an other .py file as functions.py

```
def sum(x,y):
return x+y
def average(x,y):
return (x+y)/2
def power(x,y):
return x**y
```

That's it. We have created our package called mypackage. The following is a folder structure:

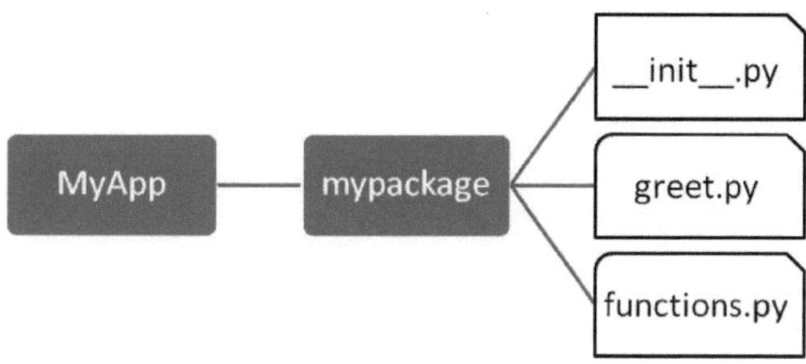

Fig-Package Folder Structure

5.7.1 Importing a Module from a Package

Now, to test our package, navigate the command prompt to the MyApp folder and invoke the Python prompt from there.

```
D:\MyApp>python
```

```
>>> from mypackage import functions
>>> functions.power(3,2)
9
```

It is also possible to import specific functions from a module in the package.

5.7.2 __init__.py

The package folder contains a special file called __init__.py, which stores the package's content. It serves two purposes: 1.The Python interpreter recognizes a folder as the package if it contains __init__.py file. 2. __init__.py exposes specified resources from its modules to be imported.

An empty __init__.py file makes all functions from the above modules available when this package is imported.

Printed by Libri Plureos GmbH in Hamburg,
Germany